# 一白水星命

## One White Life Star

## Feng Shui Essentials: Xuan Kong Nine Life Star
# ONE WHITE LIFE STAR

Copyright © 2011 by Joey Yap
All rights reserved worldwide.
First Edition July 2011

All intellectual property rights contained or in relation to this book belongs to Joey Yap.

No part of this book may be copied, used, subsumed, or exploited in fact, field of thought or general idea, by any other authors or persons, or be stored in a retrieval system, transmitted or reproduced in any way, including but not limited to digital copying and printing in any form whatsoever worldwide without the prior agreement and written permission of the author.

The author can be reached at:

**Mastery Academy of Chinese Metaphysics Sdn. Bhd. (611143-A)**
19-3, The Boulevard, Mid Valley City,
59200 Kuala Lumpur, Malaysia.
Tel       : +603-2284 8080
Fax      : +603-2284 1218
Website : www.masteryacademy.com

DISCLAIMER:

The author, Joey Yap and the publisher, JY Books Sdn Bhd, have made their best efforts to produce this high quality, informative and helpful book. They have verified the technical accuracy of the information and contents of this book. Any information pertaining to the events, occurrences, dates and other details relating to the person or persons, dead or alive, and to the companies have been verified to the best of their abilities based on information obtained or extracted from various websites, newspaper clippings and other public media. However, they make no representation or warranties of any kind with regard to the contents of this book and accept no liability of any kind for any losses or damages caused or alleged to be caused directly or indirectly from using the information contained herein.

Published by JY Books Sdn. Bhd. (659134-T)

# Table of content :

| 1 | LIFE STAR REFERENCE TABLE | 7 |
|---|---|---|
| 2 | INTRODUCTION | 12 |
| 3 | **YOUR XUAN KONG LIFE STAR** | 23 |
|   | Basic Attributes | 24 |
| 4 | **YOUR Feng Shui Essentials** | 27 |
|   | Directions | 29 |
|   | Taking the Direction using a Compass | 33 |
|   | Favorable Directions | 39 |
|   | Unfavorable Directions | 49 |
|   | Bed Alignment Direction | 58 |
|   | Best Floor | 60 |
|   | Personal Grand Duke Direction | 65 |
|   | Personal Clash Direction | 71 |
|   | Flying Star Effects | 76 |
| 5 | **THE FIVE ELEMENT** | 97 |

| 6 | **CHARACTERISTICS OF STAR** | 109 |
|---|---|---|
| | The Good | 111 |
| | The Bad | 117 |
| 7 | **CAREER AND WEALTH** | 123 |
| | Characteristics at work | 124 |
| | Suitable Job Roles | 128 |
| | Career and Wealth Guide | 132 |
| 8 | **RELATIONSHIPS** | 139 |
| | Guide for relationships | 140 |
| 9 | **HEALTH** | 145 |
| | Guide for Health | 146 |
| 10 | **COMPATIBILITY with OTHER LIFE STARS** | 151 |

# LIFE STAR REFERENCE TABLE

## Year Pillar and Gua Number Reference Table for 1912 - 2055

| Animal | Year of Birth | | | Gua Number for Male | Gua Number for Female | Year of Birth | | | Gua Number for Male | Gua Number for Female |
|---|---|---|---|---|---|---|---|---|---|---|
| Rat | 1912 | 壬子 Ren Zi | Water Rat | 7 | 8 | 1936 | 丙子 Bing Zi | Fire Rat | 1 | 5 |
| Ox | 1913 | 癸丑 Gui Chou | Water Ox | 6 | 9 | 1937 | 丁丑 Ding Chou | Fire Ox | 9 | 6 |
| Tiger | 1914 | 甲寅 Jia Yin | Wood Tiger | 5 | 1 | 1938 | 戊寅 Wu Yin | Earth Tiger | 8 | 7 |
| Rabbit | 1915 | 乙卯 Yi Mao | Wood Rabbit | 4 | 2 | 1939 | 己卯 Ji Mao | Earth Rabbit | 7 | 8 |
| Dragon | 1916 | 丙辰 Bing Chen | Fire Dragon | 3 | 3 | 1940 | 庚辰 Geng Chen | Metal Dragon | 6 | 9 |
| Snake | 1917 | 丁巳 Ding Si | Fire Snake | 2 | 4 | 1941 | 辛巳 Xin Si | Metal Snake | 5 | 1 |
| Horse | 1918 | 戊午 Wu Wu | Earth Horse | 1 | 5 | 1942 | 壬午 Ren Wu | Water Horse | 4 | 2 |
| Goat | 1919 | 己未 Ji Wei | Earth Goat | 9 | 6 | 1943 | 癸未 Gui Wei | Water Goat | 3 | 3 |
| Monkey | 1920 | 庚申 Geng Shen | Metal Monkey | 8 | 7 | 1944 | 甲申 Jia Shen | Wood Monkey | 2 | 4 |
| Rooster | 1921 | 辛酉 Xin You | Metal Rooster | 7 | 8 | 1945 | 乙酉 Yi You | Wood Rooster | 1 | 5 |
| Dog | 1922 | 壬戌 Ren Xu | Water Dog | 6 | 9 | 1946 | 丙戌 Bing Xu | Fire Dog | 9 | 6 |
| Pig | 1923 | 癸亥 Gui Hai | Water Pig | 5 | 1 | 1947 | 丁亥 Ding Hai | Fire Pig | 8 | 7 |
| Rat | 1924 | 甲子 Jia Zi | Wood Rat | 4 | 2 | 1948 | 戊子 Wu Zi | Earth Rat | 7 | 8 |
| Ox | 1925 | 乙丑 Yi Chou | Wood Ox | 3 | 3 | 1949 | 己丑 Ji Chou | Earth Ox | 6 | 9 |
| Tiger | 1926 | 丙寅 Bing Yin | Fire Tiger | 2 | 4 | 1950 | 庚寅 Geng Yin | Metal Tiger | 5 | 1 |
| Rabbit | 1927 | 丁卯 Ding Mao | Fire Rabbit | 1 | 5 | 1951 | 辛卯 Xin Mao | Metal Rabbit | 4 | 2 |
| Dragon | 1928 | 戊辰 Wu Chen | Earth Dragon | 9 | 6 | 1952 | 壬辰 Ren Chen | Water Dragon | 3 | 3 |
| Snake | 1929 | 己巳 Ji Si | Earth Snake | 8 | 7 | 1953 | 癸巳 Gui Si | Water Snake | 2 | 4 |
| Horse | 1930 | 庚午 Geng Wu | Metal Horse | 7 | 8 | 1954 | 甲午 Jia Wu | Wood Horse | 1 | 5 |
| Goat | 1931 | 辛未 Xin Wei | Metal Goat | 6 | 9 | 1955 | 乙未 Yi Wei | Wood Goat | 9 | 6 |
| Monkey | 1932 | 壬申 Ren Shen | Water Monkey | 5 | 1 | 1956 | 丙申 Bing Shen | Fire Monkey | 8 | 7 |
| Rooster | 1933 | 癸酉 Gui You | Water Rooster | 4 | 2 | 1957 | 丁酉 Ding You | Fire Rooster | 7 | 8 |
| Dog | 1934 | 甲戌 Jia Xu | Wood Dog | 3 | 3 | 1958 | 戊戌 Wu Xu | Earth Dog | 6 | 9 |
| Pig | 1935 | 乙亥 Yi Hai | Wood Pig | 2 | 4 | 1959 | 己亥 Ji Hai | Earth Pig | 5 | 1 |

- Please note that the date for the Chinese Solar Year starts on Feb 4. This means that if you were born in Feb 2 of 2002, you belong to the previous year 2001.

# Year Pillar and Gua Number Reference Table for 1912 - 2055

| Animal | Year of Birth | | | Gua Number for Male | Gua Number for Female | Year of Birth | | | Gua Number for Male | Gua Number for Female |
|---|---|---|---|---|---|---|---|---|---|---|
| Rat | 1960 | 庚子 Geng Zi | Metal Rat | 4 | 2 | 1984 | 甲子 Jia Zi | Wood Rat | 7 | 8 |
| Ox | 1961 | 辛丑 Xin Chou | Metal Ox | 3 | 3 | 1985 | 乙丑 Yi Chou | Wood Ox | 6 | 9 |
| Tiger | 1962 | 壬寅 Ren Yin | Water Tiger | 2 | 4 | 1986 | 丙寅 Bing Yin | Fire Tiger | 5 | 1 |
| Rabbit | 1963 | 癸卯 Gui Mao | Water Rabbit | 1 | 5 | 1987 | 丁卯 Ding Mao | Fire Rabbit | 4 | 2 |
| Dragon | 1964 | 甲辰 Jia Chen | Wood Dragon | 9 | 6 | 1988 | 戊辰 Wu Chen | Earth Dragon | 3 | 3 |
| Snake | 1965 | 乙巳 Yi Si | Wood Snake | 8 | 7 | 1989 | 己巳 Ji Si | Earth Snake | 2 | 4 |
| Horse | 1966 | 丙午 Bing Wu | Fire Horse | 7 | 8 | 1990 | 庚午 Geng Wu | Metal Horse | 1 | 5 |
| Goat | 1967 | 丁未 Ding Wei | Fire Goat | 6 | 9 | 1991 | 辛未 Xin Wei | Metal Goat | 9 | 6 |
| Monkey | 1968 | 戊申 Wu Shen | Earth Monkey | 5 | 1 | 1992 | 壬申 Ren Shen | Water Monkey | 8 | 7 |
| Rooster | 1969 | 己酉 Ji You | Earth Rooster | 4 | 2 | 1993 | 癸酉 Gui You | Water Rooster | 7 | 8 |
| Dog | 1970 | 庚戌 Geng Xu | Metal Dog | 3 | 3 | 1994 | 甲戌 Jia Xu | Wood Dog | 6 | 9 |
| Pig | 1971 | 辛亥 Xin Hai | Metal Pig | 2 | 4 | 1995 | 乙亥 Yi Hai | Wood Pig | 5 | 1 |
| Rat | 1972 | 壬子 Ren Zi | Water Rat | 1 | 5 | 1996 | 丙子 Bing Zi | Fire Rat | 4 | 2 |
| Ox | 1973 | 癸丑 Gui Chou | Water Ox | 9 | 6 | 1997 | 丁丑 Ding Chou | Fire Ox | 3 | 3 |
| Tiger | 1974 | 甲寅 Jia Yin | Wood Tiger | 8 | 7 | 1998 | 戊寅 Wu Yin | Earth Tiger | 2 | 4 |
| Rabbit | 1975 | 乙卯 Yi Mao | Wood Rabbit | 7 | 8 | 1999 | 己卯 Ji Mao | Earth Rabbit | 1 | 5 |
| Dragon | 1976 | 丙辰 Bing Chen | Fire Dragon | 6 | 9 | 2000 | 庚辰 Geng Chen | Metal Dragon | 9 | 6 |
| Snake | 1977 | 丁巳 Ding Si | Fire Snake | 5 | 1 | 2001 | 辛巳 Xin Si | Metal Snake | 8 | 7 |
| Horse | 1978 | 戊午 Wu Wu | Earth Horse | 4 | 2 | 2002 | 壬午 Ren Wu | Water Horse | 7 | 8 |
| Goat | 1979 | 己未 Ji Wei | Earth Goat | 3 | 3 | 2003 | 癸未 Gui Wei | Water Goat | 6 | 9 |
| Monkey | 1980 | 庚申 Geng Shen | Metal Monkey | 2 | 4 | 2004 | 甲申 Jia Shen | Wood Monkey | 5 | 1 |
| Rooster | 1981 | 辛酉 Xin You | Metal Rooster | 1 | 5 | 2005 | 乙酉 Yi You | Wood Rooster | 4 | 2 |
| Dog | 1982 | 壬戌 Ren Xu | Water Dog | 9 | 6 | 2006 | 丙戌 Bing Xu | Fire Dog | 3 | 3 |
| Pig | 1983 | 癸亥 Gui Hai | Water Pig | 8 | 7 | 2007 | 丁亥 Ding Hai | Fire Pig | 2 | 4 |

- Please note that the date for the Chinese Solar Year starts on Feb 4. This means that if you were born in Feb 2 of 2002, you belong to the previous year 2001.

玄空九星命

## Year Pillar and Gua Number Reference Table for 1912 - 2055

| Animal | Year of Birth | | | Gua Number for Male | Gua Number for Female | Year of Birth | | | Gua Number for Male | Gua Number for Female |
|---|---|---|---|---|---|---|---|---|---|---|
| Rat | 2008 | 戊子 Wu Zi | Earth Rat | 1 | 5 | 2032 | 壬子 Ren Zi | Water Rat | 4 | 2 |
| Ox | 2009 | 己丑 Ji Chou | Earth Ox | 9 | 6 | 2033 | 癸丑 Gui Chou | Water Ox | 3 | 3 |
| Tiger | 2010 | 庚寅 Geng Yin | Metal Tiger | 8 | 7 | 2034 | 甲寅 Jia Yin | Wood Tiger | 2 | 4 |
| Rabbit | 2011 | 辛卯 Xin Mao | Metal Rabbit | 7 | 8 | 2035 | 乙卯 Yi Mao | Wood Rabbit | 1 | 5 |
| Dragon | 2012 | 壬辰 Ren Chen | Water Dragon | 6 | 9 | 2036 | 丙辰 Bing Chen | Fire Dragon | 9 | 6 |
| Snake | 2013 | 癸巳 Gui Si | Water Snake | 5 | 1 | 2037 | 丁巳 Ding Si | Fire Snake | 8 | 7 |
| Horse | 2014 | 甲午 Jia Wu | Wood Horse | 4 | 2 | 2038 | 戊午 Wu Wu | Earth Horse | 7 | 8 |
| Goat | 2015 | 乙未 Yi Wei | Wood Goat | 3 | 3 | 2039 | 己未 Ji Wei | Earth Goat | 6 | 9 |
| Monkey | 2016 | 丙申 Bing Shen | Fire Monkey | 2 | 4 | 2040 | 庚申 Geng Shen | Metal Monkey | 5 | 1 |
| Rooster | 2017 | 丁酉 Ding You | Fire Rooster | 1 | 5 | 2041 | 辛酉 Xin You | Metal Rooster | 4 | 2 |
| Dog | 2018 | 戊戌 Wu Xu | Earth Dog | 9 | 6 | 2042 | 壬戌 Ren Xu | Water Dog | 3 | 3 |
| Pig | 2019 | 己亥 Ji Hai | Earth Pig | 8 | 7 | 2043 | 癸亥 Gui Hai | Water Pig | 2 | 4 |
| Rat | 2020 | 庚子 Geng Zi | Metal Rat | 7 | 8 | 2044 | 甲子 Jia Zi | Wood Rat | 1 | 5 |
| Ox | 2021 | 辛丑 Xin Chou | Metal Ox | 6 | 9 | 2045 | 乙丑 Yi Chou | Wood Ox | 9 | 6 |
| Tiger | 2022 | 壬寅 Ren Yin | Water Tiger | 5 | 1 | 2046 | 丙寅 Bing Yin | Fire Tiger | 8 | 7 |
| Rabbit | 2023 | 癸卯 Gui Mao | Water Rabbit | 4 | 2 | 2047 | 丁卯 Ding Mao | Fire Rabbit | 7 | 8 |
| Dragon | 2024 | 甲辰 Jia Chen | Wood Dragon | 3 | 3 | 2048 | 戊辰 Wu Chen | Earth Dragon | 6 | 9 |
| Snake | 2025 | 乙巳 Yi Si | Wood Snake | 2 | 4 | 2049 | 己巳 Ji Si | Earth Snake | 5 | 1 |
| Horse | 2026 | 丙午 Bing Wu | Fire Horse | 1 | 5 | 2050 | 庚午 Geng Wu | Metal Horse | 4 | 2 |
| Goat | 2027 | 丁未 Ding Wei | Fire Goat | 9 | 6 | 2051 | 辛未 Xin Wei | Metal Goat | 3 | 3 |
| Monkey | 2028 | 戊申 Wu Shen | Earth Monkey | 8 | 7 | 2052 | 壬申 Ren Shen | Water Monkey | 2 | 4 |
| Rooster | 2029 | 己酉 Ji You | Earth Rooster | 7 | 8 | 2053 | 癸酉 Gui You | Water Rooster | 1 | 5 |
| Dog | 2030 | 庚戌 Geng Xu | Metal Dog | 6 | 9 | 2054 | 甲戌 Jia Xu | Wood Dog | 9 | 6 |
| Pig | 2031 | 辛亥 Xin Hai | Metal Pig | 5 | 1 | 2055 | 乙亥 Yi Hai | Wood Pig | 8 | 7 |

- Please note that the date for the Chinese Solar Year starts on Feb 4. This means that if you were born in Feb 2 of 2002, you belong to the previous year 2001.

Xuan Kong Nine Life Star

**To download your One White Life Star Reference Chart FREE go to**

www.masteryacademy.com/regbook

Here is your unique code for access:

# GBSN6011

# Introduction

When all is said and done, Feng Shui is the study of how environments affect the people living within them. It can yield advice on which environments, at both a macro and micro level, are 'good' places or 'bad' places to live for given people at given times.

Xuan Kong is only one subsection of the study of Feng Shui and the Life Stars are only one component in the Xuan Kong Feng Shui system. This means that the study of Life Stars gives us only one piece of the overall Feng Shui puzzle but it is an important one!

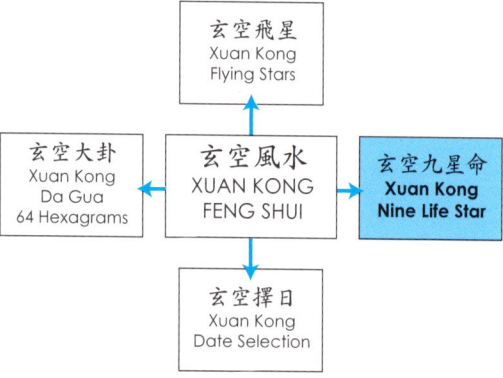

We can use the Xuan Kong Life Star system to help us with a number of practical Feng Shui and interpersonal decisions that make a big impact.

When we assess Feng Shui, we assess four factors: Environment, Buildings, Time and People. This book has been written to complement a number of other Feng Shui titles;

1. Feng Shui for Homebuyers – Exterior;
2. Feng Shui for Homebuyers – Interior;
3. Feng Shui for Apartment Buyers; and
4. Pure Feng Shui.

These other books talk about the influence of Environment, Buildings and Time on Feng Shui. This book looks at the final aspect: **People.**

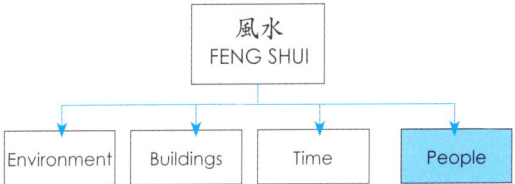

Different people will be affected in different ways by any given environment. The Life Stars directly determine what role the environment plays in the lives of its occupants. Every person is governed by one of the 9 Life Stars. These Stars also help determine key personal characteristics.

In this book, you will learn how the annually changing Xuan Kong Flying Stars interact with your Life Star so that you know what different sectors of your home will bring you. You can then use this information for your own benefit and safety. For maximum benefit, people should seek to align themselves with the direction in their home that yields positive effects. For instance, the #9 Purple Flying Star brings about the potential of career advancement for Star 1 people. Clearly this is a benefit that professionally minded people would like to take advantage of, so they may wish to spend more time absorbing the influence of the #9 Purple Flying Star in their home or place of work. The same Flying Star also indicates a heightened risk of miscarriage for pregnant women though and so pregnant Life Star 1 women should be exercise heightened caution in the presence of this Flying Star, and avoid its influence if possible.

Because the advice generated by this book on Xuan Kong Life Stars takes into account your Life Star when discussing the effects of the Flying Stars, the advice given is highly tailored to your life.

## The Positive Side Of You

Your Life Star brings a force to bear on you, wherever you are. This force can have positive or negative effects, depending on the Feng Shui of the environment you reside in.

We are all multi faceted and complex. We have good habits and bad habits; a strong side and a weak side. By correctly tapping into the right Qi your best side will manifest itself more. When you put your best foot forward more in life, more opportunities

and success comes your way. Conversely, if you find yourself under the negative influence of your Life Star, more of your negative personality traits will prevail. Your environment filters out the good or the bad influence of your Life Star. Xuan Kong Feng Shui shows us how we can align ourself to receive the best possible influence. By simply aligning your bed and study desk to correspond with your favourable Personal Directions for example, you can already take one big step towards absorbing the beneficial influence of your Life Star, even whilst you sleep and study! If you are choosing a new home then choosing the correct floor at the correct time will bring further benefits. Avoiding your Personal Grand Duke and Crash Sectors will keep health problems and conflict at bay.

Does all of this mean you must tip-toe around certain rooms in your house or seal them off? No. Feng Shui does not need to become all consuming. If you can easily align your bed so that you receive benefits then why not do so? There are real world limits to what can be done, it is not practical, for instance, to rebuild your home if it does not perfectly cater to the instructions that this book gives. Your ideal floor choice in a condominium may not be available. The list of real world complications goes on.

You can tailor Feng Shui to work for you; making smaller, simple changes so that you reap the maximum possible benefit. The pursuit of good Feng Shui is not intended to take up all of your time and this flexible book is perfect for anyone, no matter how busy or restricted you are in your decisions.

## Your Life Star

Everyone falls under the jurisdiction of one of the 9 Life Stars and this will have different consequences for everyone. Your Life Star describes your key skills, characteristics and traits. Some people are creative but reserved, some people are aggressive and driven. What self destructive traits do you have? Do you have a bloated sense of pride or are you prone to gossip? Your Life Star can shine some light on the complexity of your personality and your good and bad traits.

Study of the Life Stars has practical benefits for everyone; it gives you valuable information about others in addition to yourself. Different Life Stars bestow different abilities on people which means that people belonging to each Star will exhibit different characteristics at work. A Star 1 person is diplomatic so they are best suited to roles demanding diplomacy, for example. Accordingly, employers can study the Xuan Kong Life Stars when making work place decisions whilst employees can use the system to help them go about working productively with their colleagues and superiors, even when disagreements arise.

If you become aware of your own harmful tendencies then you can learn to minimize them so you can advance. Similar benefits can be seen in romantic relationships and friendships. Learning that a Star

7 individual needs their space and independence might help you accommodate this in your dealings with them when you might otherwise have been tempted to be clingy and dependant.

When we understand more about ourselves we can stop ourselves from making mistakes and perhaps forgive certain behaviour in others once we understand where it comes from.

## Compatibility Guide

Certain people are, of course, more compatible with each other than others. In partnerships or relationships this takes on a new level of importance. Different Life Stars bestow the qualities of different elements on different people; for example, a Star 1 person has the qualities of water whilst a Star 7 person has the qualities of the Yin Metal element. Just as the elements control, pacify and weaken one another, individuals of the different Stars may dominate, clash with or enrich one another. This book includes a write up of how compatible different Stars are with one another. You may find that a relationship as a Star 1 person with a Star 5 person simply isn't worth the effort. A compatibility guide on each interaction gives you tips on how to best deal with the other Stars for mutual benefit, even taking into account your differences.

## Compatible With BaZi Profiling Systems

If you are familiar with the **BaZi Profiling System** then you will be aware that, at first glance, it seems to deal with very similar issues. It can tell us about other preferences and internal view of the world. Do we have an optimistic view of things? Do we blame ourselves too much?

While there is some overlap between the jurisdiction of the Xuan Kong Life Star system and BaZi Profiling System, they are two different systems. They both deal with individual people and their personalities but they are not mutually exclusive. In fact, when studied together, they can be thought of as two pieces of the same puzzle.

The BaZi Profiling System tells us about ourselves and about others. It even tells us things that cannot be observed about others (things people do not communicate). What it can't tell us is how the outside environment plays into the picture. The Xuan Kong Nine Stars help determine *which* qualities are brought out and by what features and external forms in the environment.

Once we know what directions are conducive to good Qi, how external forms (pylons etc) can compound problems related to sectors in the home, which areas of our environment increase the risk of which ailments or even which people can create problems in our lives (compatibility guide) then we can begin shaping our external environment to whatever degree necessary in order to enjoy the most

happiness, wealth and success. Xuan Kong Feng Shui tells you precisely what effect the environment and compass directions will have on which people.

If you are simply interested in learning what makes a person tick rather than making decisions about an ideal environment for them to thrive in then I recommend you take up further study of the BaZi Profiling System. The goal of BaZi is to pinpoint personal deficiencies so that they may be overcome or to highlight personal strengths so that they may be capitalised on.

If you are trying to configure your environment in order to maximize the benefits that your home or place of work bestow upon you in terms of health, wealth and relationships, then the Feng Shui Xuan Kong Life Star system is the one for you.

When you combine the two systems and employ them on yourself you will be able to make the most of your best qualities and then seek out an environment which lets you shine and gives the least resistance. A powerful combination of self improvement and informed decision making!

## An Easier Life

Life doesn't have to be difficult. It is possible to effectively dodge conflict, problem situations and health problems if you know they are coming. The Life Stars hold the key to many of the "surprises" that life has in store for us and we can learn to shape our environment to our own advantage. This is exciting stuff! Seeking out the best romantic relationships and business opportunities is a top priority for most people and the power of your Life Star can be called upon in these pursuits.

Even though much is made of the layout of the home with relation to Feng Shui, you won't need to bend over backwards to accommodate the advice given in this book. For instance, where you cannot choose the ideal living floor specified, second and third choices are mentioned. You can take as much or as little from this book as you need without fear of it making you paranoid and prey to "paralysis by analysis". Looking back on your own life, you can most probably think of two or three big mistakes – a bad business deal or choice in romantic partner, perhaps. Avoiding pitfalls of this magnitude in the future is made a whole lot easier when you have some idea of how likely they are to occur. If you can make changes to your environment to further reduce this likelihood then all the better!

I hope that this book expands your world view. Once you know how to utilize them, the Nine Stars can be the harbinger of great fortune instead of misery for you. If you can stay on the 'correct side' of your Star and always position yourself to bask in its positive influence then many happy successes await you.

Joey Yap
2011

 www.facebook.com/joeyyapFB

**Author's personal website :**
www.joeyyap.com

**Academy websites :**
www.masteryacademy.com | www.maelearning.com | www.baziprofiling.com

# 一白水星命

## One White Life Star

| Life Star 1 | Born in |
|---|---|
| Male | 1927, 1936, 1945, 1954, 1963 1972, 1981, 1990, 1999, 2008 |
| Female | 1923, 1932, 1941, 1950, 1959 1968, 1977, 1986, 1995, 2004 |

- Please note that the date for the Chinese Solar Year starts on Feb 4. This means that if you were born in Feb 2 of 2002, you belong to the previous year 2001.

# Your Xuan Kong Life Star

Your Xuan Kong Life Star is Gua #1, and your trigram is called Kan. It looks like this:

For the rest of this book, we will refer to your Gua 1 as **Life Star 1**.

# Basic Attributes of Star 1

Your Star 1, being of the Water element, will share some of the traits of Water. There are two types of Water Qi that we must think of here: still and moving. We all know that still water runs deep, and as such you have the potential to be reticent, secretive, and introverted. At the same time, 1 is the most Yang number, and so you can also gush strongly, as in the water that runs through the mouth of a river or the waves that crash onto the beach. You tend to have a certain duality to your nature.

Like water, you can become colourless and adapt freely and flexibly to whatever is around you. This characteristic also means that you tend to seek out the path of least resistance in life, which can make you ineffectual or vague when it comes to dealing with actual obstacles and problems. You do not seek out conflict. On your own terms, you are good at "going with the flow" and finding your own way. You always find solutions to your problems eventually. Creativity, adaptability, and intelligence are your hallmark traits.

On the other hand, your fast-moving nature can bring out aggression, making you unstoppable and impatient to the point of weakness. This can result in a display of bad temper, which is also accompanied by your rather volatile changes of mood that can go from good to bad in a very short time, or vice versa. Because you think that there is a solution to every problem, you can be impulsive, rash, and unrealistic. You can also be very sensitive, although you tend to hide your thin skin quite well sometimes so that it takes others by surprise when you do show that you have been hurt.

### Basic Emotions & Temperament

**Plus :** Reflective, insightful, courageous, independent, explorative, adaptable

**Minus:** Manipulative, stubborn, defensive, paranoid, overbearing

風水

# YOUR FENG SHUI ESSENTIALS

The Feng Shui Essentials comprise Feng Shui Directions, the effects of the Xuan Kong Nine Stars in various sectors and areas of your home and workspace, and the Five Elements.

Each of these factors interact with your Life Star in different ways that will affect how your Life Star manifests itself and determine whether or not it brings out good or bad qualities in you.

方向

# Directions

# Directions

Direction is an integral component of understanding the Nine Life Stars. Different directions in your home and your place of work can either accentuate or depreciate the strength of your Life Star.

Favorable Direction will highlight or enhance the positive traits of your Life Star, while an Unfavorable Direction will diminish or weaken your Life Star and bring out some of its negative attributes.

The Life Star numbers are categorized into two groups: the East Group and the West Group. The names 'East Group' and 'West Group' are just to demarcate the Greater and Lesser Yin transformation of the Tai Ji. They do not literally represent directions.

East Group Life Stars include 1, 3, 4 and 9. Those who are Life Stars 2, 6, 7 and 8 belong to the West Group. The following table will give you a quick reference of the Auspicious and Inauspicious compass directions of the East and West Group.

## East Group 東命

| 卦<br>Gua | 生氣<br>Shen Qi<br>Life Generating | 天醫<br>Tian Yi<br>Heavenly Doctor | 延年<br>Yan Nian<br>Longevity | 伏位<br>Fu Wei<br>Stability | 禍害<br>Huo Hai<br>Mishaps | 五鬼<br>Wu Gui<br>Five Ghosts | 六煞<br>Liu Sha<br>Six Killings | 絕命<br>Jue Ming<br>Life Threatening |
|---|---|---|---|---|---|---|---|---|
| 坎<br>Kan<br>1 Water | 東南<br>South East | 東<br>East | 南<br>South | 北<br>North | 西<br>West | 東北<br>North East | 西北<br>North West | 西南<br>South West |
| 震<br>Zhen<br>3 Wood | 南<br>South | 北<br>North | 東南<br>South East | 東<br>East | 西南<br>South West | 西北<br>North West | 東北<br>North East | 西<br>West |
| 巽<br>Xun<br>4 Wood | 北<br>North | 南<br>South | 東<br>East | 東南<br>South East | 西北<br>North West | 西南<br>South West | 西<br>West | 東北<br>North East |
| 離<br>Li<br>9 Fire | 東<br>East | 東南<br>South East | 北<br>North | 南<br>South | 東北<br>North East | 西<br>West | 西南<br>South West | 西北<br>North West |

## West Group 西命

| 卦<br>Gua | 生氣<br>Shen Qi<br>Life Generating | 天醫<br>Tian Yi<br>Heavenly Doctor | 延年<br>Yan Nian<br>Longevity | 伏位<br>Fu Wei<br>Stability | 禍害<br>Huo Hai<br>Mishaps | 五鬼<br>Wu Gui<br>Five Ghosts | 六煞<br>Liu Sha<br>Six Killings | 絕命<br>Jue Ming<br>Life Threatening |
|---|---|---|---|---|---|---|---|---|
| 坤<br>Kun<br>2 Earth | 東北<br>North East | 西<br>West | 西北<br>North West | 西南<br>South West | 東<br>East | 東南<br>South East | 南<br>South | 北<br>North |
| 乾<br>Qian<br>6 Metal | 西<br>West | 東北<br>North East | 西南<br>South West | 西北<br>North West | 東南<br>South East | 東<br>East | 北<br>North | 南<br>South |
| 兌<br>Dui<br>7 Metal | 西北<br>North West | 西南<br>South West | 東北<br>North East | 西<br>West | 北<br>North | 南<br>South | 東南<br>South East | 東<br>East |
| 艮<br>Gen<br>8 Earth | 西南<br>South West | 西北<br>North West | 西<br>West | 東北<br>North East | 南<br>South | 北<br>North | 東<br>East | 東南<br>South East |

The concepts of Favorable and Unfavorable are derived from the Eight Wandering Stars system of the Ba Zhai Eight Mansion Feng Shui 八宅風水.

Each of the 8 directions is governed by a Star. These Wandering Stars will affect each Xuan Kong Life Star in different ways. Each Life Star has four Favorable Directions governed by Auspicious Stars: Sheng Qi 生氣 (Life Generating), Tian Yi 天醫 (Heavenly Doctor), Yan Nian 延年 (Longevity), and Fu Wei 伏位 (Stability).

The four Unfavorable Directions are governed by Inauspicious Stars and include Huo Hai 禍害 (Mishaps), Wu Gui 五鬼 (Five Ghost), Liu Sha 六煞 (Six Killings) and Jue Ming 絕命 (Life Diminishing).

The following are the Favorable and Unfavorable Directions for Star 1.

# Taking the Direction using a Compass

You will need a compass – or alternatively, the Joey Yap iLuoPan app for iPhone available at the Apple App Store – to determine the direction of your Main Door, Bed and Stove. Hold your compass or iLuoPan at waist level as shown on the illustration below. Your compass or iLuoPan will align to the magnetic North on its own. All you need to know is how to take your direction as indicated on the following pages.

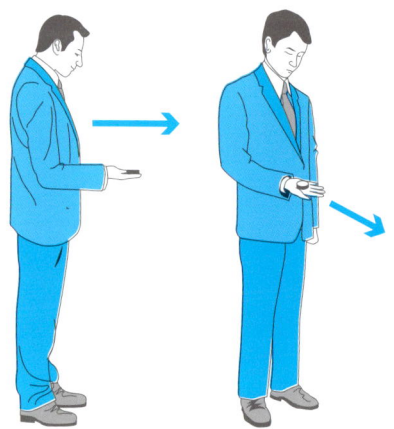

## Facing Direction of the Main Door

1. Stand about one foot outside the door looking outwards.

2. Use the square base of your compass to help you align yourself parallel to the door.

3. Read the facing direction on your compass.

# Facing Direction of the Bed

1. Measure from the head of the bed where your head is placed when you lie down (the direction the headboard faces) and not the direction your feet face.

# Facing Direction of the Stove

1. For modern (gas or electric) stoves, look at the where direction of the cooking knobs (fire igniters) are pointing to determine its facing direction.

2. For traditional stoves that require wood and fire to work, look for their 'fire mouth' as the facing direction.

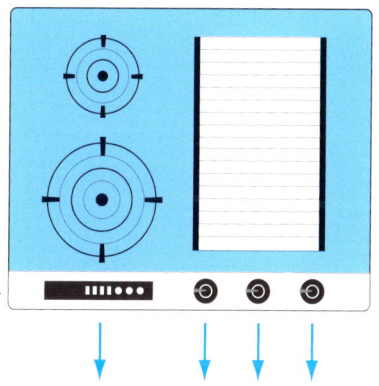

# Favorable Directions

# Southeast
# 東南 (127.6°-142.5°)

## Life Generating
## 生氣 *(Sheng Qi)*

**The basic characteristics of the Sheng Qi Star:**

It brings about promotions, career advancements, strong money and wealth luck, potential political power and authority, and all-round success.

The Sheng Qi Star represents life-generating Qi or energy. It also represents the Wood Element, and hence, governs the facets of success, authority, nobility, status and wealth in life. Wood relates to growth and advancement in life, and as such is an extremely auspicious Star to tap into. For you, the Southeast direction taps into the Sheng Qi potential.

This Star is suitable for business (commercial), career and wealth-related pursuits. It would therefore be ideal for a business or residence to have its Main Door situated in the Sheng Qi sector as it allows you to tap into these energies to create opportunities for profit and long term wealth opportunities.

Sheng Qi is an active star by nature and thus, it is not conducive for rest or sleep-related activities. It is best to avoid having the bed or bedroom located in this sector or for anyone to sleep facing this direction. Use this sector for your work or for active pursuits instead of relaxing ones.

If this sector is missing from a house or is lacking in the office or the premises of a business, the wealth-related aspects of your career or venture will be considerably weakened and it will be a difficult struggle to amass wealth and prosperity.

# East
東 (82.6°-97.5°)

## Heavenly Doctor
天醫 *(Tian Yi)*

 **The basic characteristics of the Tian Yi Star:**

It brings about general good luck and well-being, as well as positive mentor luck or the presence of sound advisors and guidance.

This Star represents the Earth Element and is therefore the determinant of noble people (mentors) and people of caliber and status. It also denotes your health prospects and physical wellbeing. As such, the Tian Yi Star is best utilised to help generate guidance for your career or for any project which you've embarked upon. It will bring about the help and assistance of others.

It is also a useful Star for health purposes, and its benefits can be employed when you need to recuperate, recover, or heal from an illness, surgical procedure or health issue.

When the Tian Yin sector is missing from a home or office, your health is likely to suffer because of it. In addition, you will also find help from noble people hard to come by, especially in times of need in life and career matters. You will come across more obstacles and obstructions which you must overcome on your own without the external help of others.

Since the Tian Yi Star represents nobility, it also governs your reputation, respectability, and your oratory powers. It thus has influence on your powers of speech and persuasion, and has some bearing on how you are perceived by others and how well they respond to your verbal overtures.

# South
南 (172.6°-187.5°)

## Longevity
延年 *(Yan Nian)*

**The basic characteristics of the Yan Nian Star:**

It prolongs and enhances life and improves the quality of your life. It promotes good communication with others which in turn makes for good relationships.

The Yan Nian Star represents the Metal Element, and as such governs speech and the effectiveness of your words. If you are looking to establish good relationships and rapport with others, you will need the help of this Star, since it governs aspects of successful networking, communication and relationship building.

The Yan Nian Star is important for family harmony and domestic bliss. It is also necessary if you wish to build good relationships with co-workers and colleagues. Essentially, it paves the way for smooth interpersonal relations, seldom plagued by misunderstanding, arguments and flare-ups. As such, the presence of the Yan Nian Star is useful for maintaining harmony.

If you are employed in public relations or marketing and you must interact with clients and customers as part of your daily routine, you will find the Qi brought about by this Star very useful to your career.

Do note that if the Yan Nian sector is missing, harmony and unity will be adversely affected, and relations are likely to be tense or strained. At the very least, you can expect more argument and discord with others.

# North
# 北 (352.6°-7.5°)

## Stability
## 伏位 (Fu Wei)

 **The basic characteristics of the Fu Wei Star:**

It is a Star that promotes calm and keeps you grounded. It allows for peace of mind and rationality. It also promotes good luck.

The Fu Wei Star represents the Wood Element. When qualities or virtues such as calmness and tranquility are required, this is the Star you need! It promotes peace of mind and heightens clarity of thought, so this is also the Star to use if you need to focus, study or make important decisions.

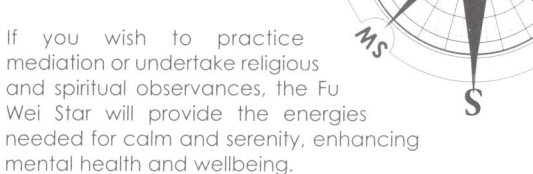

If you wish to practice mediation or undertake religious and spiritual observances, the Fu Wei Star will provide the energies needed for calm and serenity, enhancing mental health and wellbeing.

This Star is most suitably applied to libraries, study areas/zones or other places where concentration is necessary. When considering the home or workplace, this Star can help create areas where the mind can be easily quietened and people can reflect and turn inward.

When the Fu Wei sector is missing from a place, peace of mind will be difficult to attain.

# Unfavorable Directions

# West
西 (262.6°-277.5°)

## Mishaps
禍害 (Huo Hai)

**The basic characteristics of the Huo Hai Star:** It denotes potential calamities, accidents, and mishaps. It undermines good efforts and brings about the risk of mistakes and errors.

The Huo Hai Star represents the Earth Element and is the harbinger of mishaps, loss of wealth, sudden (unfortunate) changes or hassles as well as work-related obstacles. What it does is undermine your efforts and bring about sudden obstructions or problems that will result in a loss of time and energy.

If, for example, the Main Door of a property is located in this direction, you can reasonably expect to encounter quite a few obstacles and problems in your daily life. It is best to work around this area particularly if your main door or office is located in the West sector.

The detrimental effects of a negative star are compounded when it is located within an area that is already affected by negative Feng Shui, so pay attention to the negative structures outside this area.

# Northeast
東北 (37.6°-52.5°)

## Five Ghosts
五鬼 (Wu Gui)

**The basic characteristics of the Wu Gui Star:**

It brings about betrayal and treachery through back-stabbing, gossip, and rumours. It also denotes endless bickering and fraught tension brought about by arguments.

The Wu Gui Star represents the Fire Element and is the bringer of betrayal, ill-intentioned gossip, rumours, backstabbing, cruelty, petty people and even subterfuge and sabotage. It generally denotes a sense of unease brought upon by less-than-honest speech.

The presence of Wu Gui in a house causes disloyalty and discord amongst family members, affecting relationships and marriages. If it is present in your work place, then you should also watch out for fights and arguments between your colleagues or subordinates and friction or tension with your superiors.

Negative external forms such as (sharp) pylons and jagged rooftops pointing towards a house further aggravate the effects of this Star.

# Northwest
## 西北 (307.6°-322.5°)

### Six Killings
### 六煞 (Liu Sha)

**The basic characteristics of the Liu Sha Star:**

This Star brings about injuries and accidents. It also denotes the possibility of betrayals and dishonesty, and the risk of potential scandals.

The Liu Sha Star relates to the element of Water and is the harbinger of lawsuits and potential scandals. Legal problems at the workplace or adulterous affairs in relation to your marriage or personal relationships could be brought to light.

This Star is also the Harbinger of bodily injury, harm and conditions requiring people to undergo physical surgery. Robberies and theft are also likely, and you will have to be careful about what information you share with others and with the general safety of your personal documents and possessions.

Be mindful of the presence of negative external forms, which will compound the adverse effects of this Star. For instance, a Y-shaped road at the Liu Sha sector will result in scandalous affairs, while negative structures as mentioned earlier will compound and exacerbate the harmful effects of the Liu Sha Star.

# Southwest
# 西南 (217.6°-232.5°)

## Life Threatening
## 絕命 (Jue Ming)

**The basic characteristics of the Jue Ming Star:**

It brings about the risk of accidents and major illness, and the threat of miscarriage for pregnant women. It also signals potential for great calamity.

This star represents the Metal Element and it signifies accidents and illnesses. The energies of the Jue Ming Star are quite severe and so are it's adverse effects, bringing with it considerable risk.

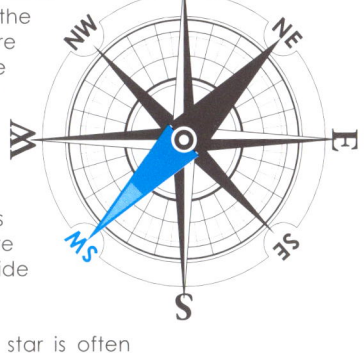

In severe cases, the Jue Ming Star can even cause fatal accidents, ailments or injuries when there are negative external forms outside of the Southwest sector.

It is to no surprise that this star is often regarded as the primary star of misfortune and calamity in the study of Ba Zhai Feng Shui. Other than catastrophes and accidents, it can also cause major loss of wealth and theft as well as the cause of breakups or separation in relationships.

# Bed Alignment Direction

One of the key Feng Shui factors of the bedroom is how your bed is placed. For starters, your bed should preferably be pushed against a wall, with the headboard flush with the wall. The most important thing you can do when laying out your bedroom with regards to Feng Shui is to make sure your headboard is aligned with your Favorable Direction.

Facing Direction, in the case of bed alignment, refers to the direction of your headboard. This means it is the direction your head faces when you lie down on the bed, and **not** the direction that your feet face.

As a Star 1, your Bed Alignment Directions are:

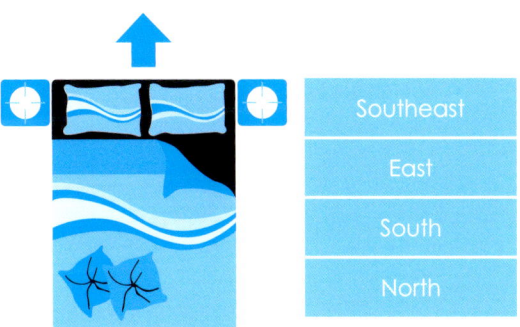

# Best Floor

A reality of modern life is that most of us do not live in houses these days, instead living in multi story apartments and condominium blocks.

Some of us are pretty mobile and live a nomad-like lifestyle that may require us to stay in high-rise buildings for certain periods of time. As such, it becomes important to select the right floor to reside in. The objective of this is to achieve elemental affinity between you (the occupant) with the energies of a particular floor.

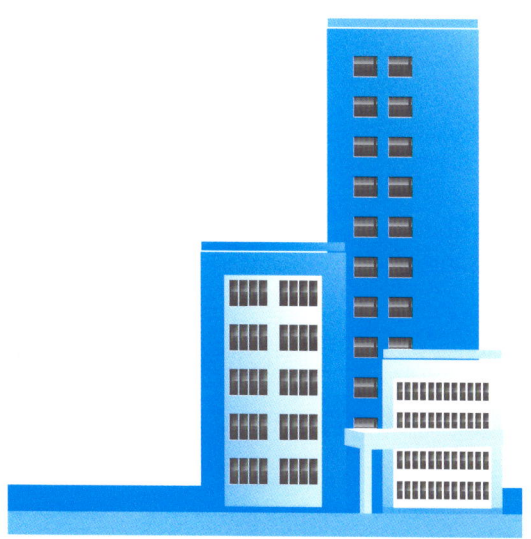

As you are a Star 1 person of the Water element, the chart below describes the best floors for you to live on in terms of first choice, second choice, and third choice.

| First Choice | Second Choice | Third Choice |
|---|---|---|
| 1st Floor | 4th Floor | 2nd floor |
| 6th Floor | 9th Floor | 7th floor |
| 11th Floor | 14th Floor | 12th Floor |
| 16th Floor | 19th Floor | 17th floor |
| 21st Floor | 24th Floor | 22nd Floor |
| 26th Floor | 29th Floor | 27th floor |
| 31st Floor | 34th Floor | 32nd Floor |
| 36th Floor | 39th Floor | 37th floor |
| 41st Floor | 44th Floor | 42nd Floor |
| 46th Floor | 49th Floor | 49th Floor |

**Select :**
Metal and Water
Building Shapes

**Avoid :**
Earth and Wood
Building Shapes

# Personal Grand Duke Directions

Identifying the Grand Duke Sector is important. Your Personal Grand Duke Sector relates to your birth year. For example, if you are born in the year of the rat then the rat is your Personal Grand Duke and we know that the Rat sector is North 2.

We want to avoid the harmful properties of this area and as you are a Star 1 person, you can locate your Personal Grand Duke Sector in the following directions:

## Personal Grand Duke Directions for Male

| MALE Birth Year | Personal Grand Duke | Direction |
|---|---|---|
| 1918, 1954, 1990, 2026 | 午 Wu Horse | 南2 South 2 |
| 1927, 1963, 1999, 2035 | 卯 Mao Rabbit | 東2 East 2 |
| 1936, 1972, 2008, 2044 | 子 Zi Rat | 北2 North 2 |
| 1945, 1981, 2017, 2053 | 酉 You Rooster | 西2 West 2 |

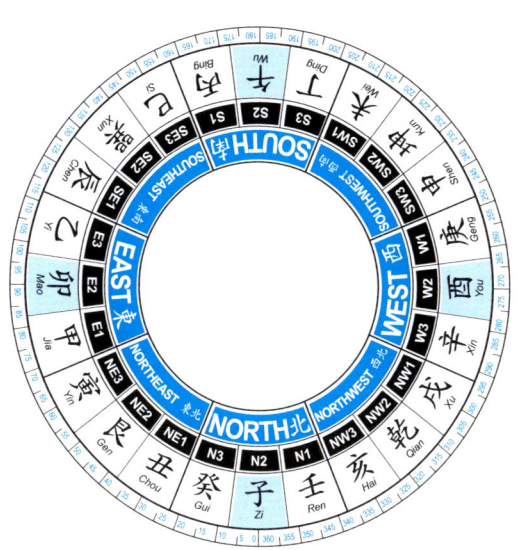

## Personal Grand Duke Directions for Female

| FEMALE<br>Birth Year | Personal<br>Grand Duke | Direction |
|---|---|---|
| 1914, 1950, 1986, 2022 | 寅<br>Yin<br>Tiger | 東北 3<br>Northeast 3 |
| 1923, 1959, 1995, 2031 | 亥<br>Hai<br>Pig | 西北 3<br>Northwest 3 |
| 1932, 1968, 2004, 2040 | 申<br>Shen<br>Monkey | 西南 3<br>Southwest 3 |
| 1941, 1977, 2013, 2049 | 巳<br>Si<br>Snake | 東南 3<br>Southeast 3 |

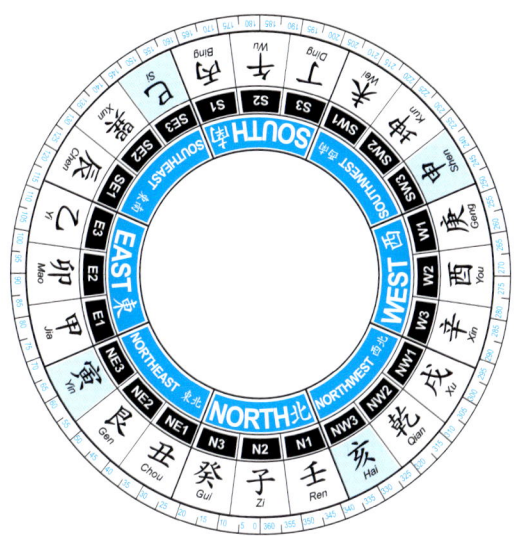

Ideally, you should not have a bathroom or toilet located in these areas of your home above and Sha Qi external features such as pylons, T-junctions, Dead Tree should be avoided. The Sha Qi in the Personal Grand Duke Sector is extremely strong and so all efforts to avoid spending a lot of time in it should be made. It goes without saying that the Personal Grand Duke Sector of your home is not the ideal spot for a bedroom! The Sha Qi in this area of the home is so strong in fact that it is difficult for any further negative Qi to enter!

# Personal Clash Directions

Your home will contain Personal Clash Sectors. Spending time in these areas of your home will bring up problems in your life with significant others. As a Star 1 person, you will find your Personal Clash Sectors in the following directions:

### Personal Clash Directions for Male

| MALE Birth Year | Personal Clash Sector | Direction |
|---|---|---|
| 1918, 1954, 1990, 2026 | 子 Zi Rat | 北2 North 2 |
| 1927, 1963, 1999, 2035 | 酉 You Rooster | 西2 West 2 |
| 1936, 1972, 2008, 2044 | 午 Wu Horse | 南2 South 2 |
| 1945, 1981, 2017, 2053 | 卯 Mao Rabbit | 東2 East 2 |

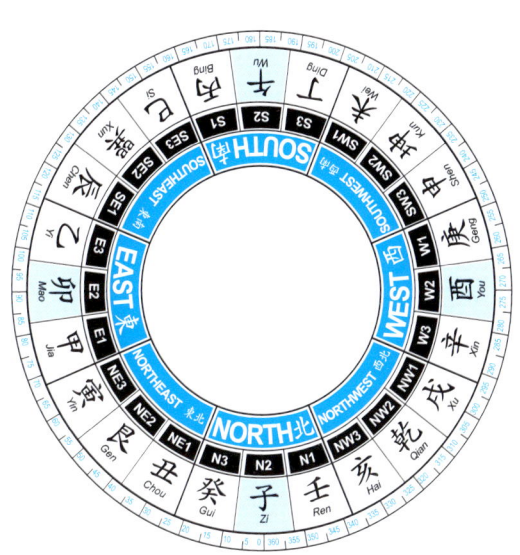

## Personal Clash Directions for Female

| FEMALE Birth Year | Personal Grand Duke | Direction |
|---|---|---|
| 1914, 1950, 1986, 2022 | 申 *Shen* **Monkey** | 西南3 **Southwest 3** |
| 1923, 1959, 1995, 2031 | 巳 *Si* **Snake** | 東南3 **Southeast 3** |
| 1932, 1968, 2004, 2040 | 寅 *Yin* **Tiger** | 東北3 **Northeast 3** |
| 1941, 1977, 2013, 2049 | 亥 *Hai* **Pig** | 西北3 **Northwest 3** |

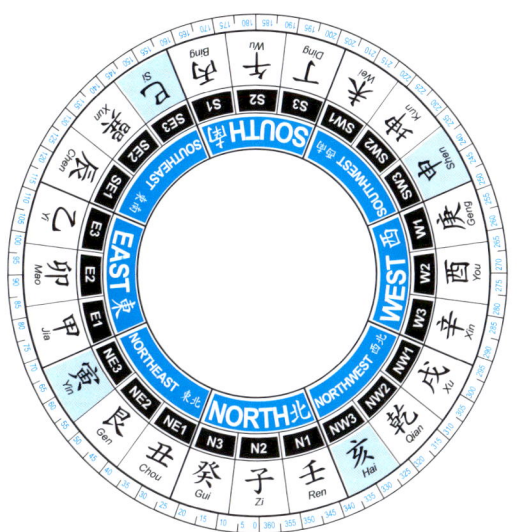

The locations above are a bad place for important features of your home such as the main door, bedroom and kitchen. You should seek to avoid these sectors in the same way you avoid your Personal Grand Duke Sector.

# Flying Stars Effects

Each year, the Xuan Kong Flying Stars fly into a different section of a property, be it your residence or your work space. The effects that these Nine Stars have on you will be different depending on your Life Star. In this section you can find out how different Flying Stars in different sectors will effect you with regards to Feng Shui.

The Flying Stars have both negative and positive attributes, but which facets will show when you see a particular star, depends on the timeliness and the period.

A few of the Nine Stars are inherently negative, a few are inherently positive in nature and some can be both good and bad. Even then, we must remember that the stars have the capacity to manifest either their positive or negative facets because in Feng Shui, nothing is ever inherently bad or good forever.

When it comes to Flying Stars, it is important to remember this key principle: Forms activate the Stars and the Stars in turn influence the People. This is what you should keep in mind as you read about the effects of the Nine Stars on your Life Star.

# 1 ⭐ → 1 White Life

The effects of the visiting **#1 White Star** on a **1 White Life:**

In terms of Feng Shui effects, a Star 1 person who lives in a sector of a home inhabited by the energy of the #1 White Star will experience an increased probability of extramarital love affairs and romantic encounters. The #1 White Star can make both men and women more likely to stray. To counter it's effects, they should be aware of the #1 White Star's influence and exercise more self discipline accordingly. Health issues include problems affecting the bowels, kidneys, and bladder. The influence of #1 White increases the risk of alcoholism, particularly in Star 1 men. There is also the risk that members of the household may have run-ins with the law, and there is the chance of robbery and theft. On the other hand, this combination is very good for academic pursuits, and will benefit those who are in scholarly and research activities or education-based projects.

# 2★ → 1 White Life

The effects of the visiting **#2 Black Star** on a **1 White Life**:

In terms of Feng Shui effects, Star 1 men residing in the area of the home influenced by the #2 Black Star may develop stomach, intestinal, and digestive problems. Women may develop stomach and gynaecological problems. As such, enhanced vigilance is called for: medical attention should be sought promptly for any concerns before they develop into the serious problems affecting the areas of the body outlined above.

Star 1 males who are married and reside in a sector with the #2 Black present will find that this combination results in some marital trouble and turbulence. This combination can lead women or wives to become an increasingly authoritative or dominant force in their relationship or family, possibly creating a power struggle, friction or conflict with their spouse.

# 3★ → 1 White Life

The effects of the visiting **#3 Jade Star** on a **1 White Life**:

In terms of Feng Shui effects, the presence of #3 Jade in your home or work sector can bring with it an increased occurrence of fights, arguments, and disputes. On the domestic front, this could mean that tempers flare on a regular basis. If the #3 Jade is present in a sector of the office, it can lead to arguments and even potential lawsuits brought about by rigid and unyielding differences in position. There is also the risk of robbery and theft if #3 Jade is present in any of the sectors, so you'll have to be more careful with your personal belongings and important documents. Fear not, there is some good news, however: the presence of #3 Jade brings about the potential for travel as well as good business and personal opportunities whilst you are on said travels.

# 4★ → 1 White Life

## The effects of the visiting #4 Green Star on a 1 White Life:

In terms of Feng Shui effects, the presence of the #4 Green in a particular sector is actually good for your academic and learning luck. You will find that it aids your concentration and helps you achieve a state of mind conducive to learning. As such, all scholarly and research activities are likely to go well and produce good results for you. When the #4 Green is a negative presence, however, it brings the potential for betrayal and treachery in a marriage or a romantic relationship. This is particularly true when there is a negative structure outside of this particular sector like a curved road facing the sector, or the presence of a structure or building with sharp edges like a pylon. Be aware of this risk when pursuing your romantic interests.

# 5★ → 1 White Life

## The effects of the visiting #5 Yellow Star on a 1 White Life:

In terms of Feng Shui effects, the presence of #5 Yellow in any area of your home or work place will lead to quite a lot of negative effects as far as your health is concerned. In particular, you will suffer from constant illness and a weakened immune system and you will find your energy levels to be low. You may not be able to perform at your optimum level. Further health problems involving your stomach and digestive system can arise, and food poisoning and stomach flu will be regular, recurring issues. In more serious instances, pregnant Star 1 women may encounter complications with their pregnancy. Women are at greater risk for uterine cancer. Venereal diseases are also a risk with the presence of #5 Yellow.

# 6 ★ → 1 White Life

The effects of the visiting **#6 White Star** on a **1 White Life:**

In terms of Feng Shui effects, the presence of #6 White in the home or work sector bodes well for you if you're in the armed forces or in some form of work pertaining to security. It is also extremely beneficial for a Star 1 person involved in literary pursuits, so if you're a creative writer the presence of #6 White will be a boon for your projects. When #6 White is in a negative form, watch out for accidents and mishaps involving sharp objects and metal implements: be careful when dealing with knives and scissors. If there are negative forms outside the sector with #6 White present, such as trees with dead, sharp branches pointing inward, then you will have to be alert to the possibility of head or brain-related injuries.

# 7★ → 1 White Life

The effects of the visiting **#7 Red Star** on a **1 White Life:**

In terms of Feng Shui effects, the presence of #7 Red in the home or work sector activates the love energy, bringing about potential romantic dalliances or relationships. This is a positive development if you're single, but if you're married or in a relationship then this could prove to be a problem that you need to circumvent somehow. In a positive form, the #7 Red bodes well for your travel activities. In a negative form, the presence of #7 Red in a particular sector that you use on a regular basis could result in the presence of sweet-talking swindlers or people who are out to take you for a ride! As such, be less trusting and handle yourself with care around strangers who seem too good to be true.

# 8★ → 1 White Life

The effects of the visiting **#8 White Star** on a **1 White Life**:

In terms of Feng Shui effects, the presence of #8 White in the home or work sector brings about some health problems and issues with your physical wellbeing. Problems involving your ears and hearing may present themselves. The presence of Star 8 for you can also lead to other forms of illness, like painful kidney stones. Pay more attention to your health when #8 White is present. However, there are positive ramifications of #8 White in terms of literary or scholarly pursuits. Those of you who are writers or in university and graduate school may benefit from the presence of #8 White. There is also a good chance that financial success is in store for you, so utilize #8 White's power if you run a business or want to boost your profits.

# 9★ → 1 White Life

The effects of the visiting **#9 Purple Star** on a **1 White Life:**

In terms of Feng Shui effects, the presence of #9 Purple in the home or work sector indicates possible sexual or extramarital dalliances that will not end well, as it brings about some health risks and potential disease. Pregnant Star 1 women using a sector with #9 Purple present should be aware for the possibility of miscarriage or some form of serious pregnancy complication. Health issues involving the heart and cardiac system can arise. Health problems aside, the presence of #9 Purple bodes well for your professional and career aspirations. If your place of work is under the influence of #9 Purple, this could result in a possible promotion or career advancement. There will be recognition of your talents and contribution, and an elevation of your status in terms of your career and your profession.

五行

# THE FIVE ELEMENTS

# The Five Elements

The element of your Life Star 1 is Water, and it is important that you understand the implications of this. In the study of Chinese Metaphysics and Feng Shui, a basic understanding of the Five Elements is integral to success. This section will briefly outline the role of the Five Elements.

The Five Elements are symbolic representations of energy, or Qi. In Feng Shui and in BaZi, the Five Elements are Earth, Metal, Water, Wood, and Fire. Water represents wisdom, thoughts, and intelligence. Its properties are that it runs or flows downhill, and is free and unbound and can fill any shape or space it is in. To visualise Water, think of waves and movement. Water is also associated with the colours blue and black, and the season of winter. Water also represents wealth.

In order to understand the elements, it's important to understand their relationship to one another. Each element does not exist in isolation. As such, these elements share three important relationships known as 'cycles' that are fundamental to the understanding of Feng Shui: the Productive Cycle, the Controlling Cycle, and the Weakening Cycle.

## Productive Cycle

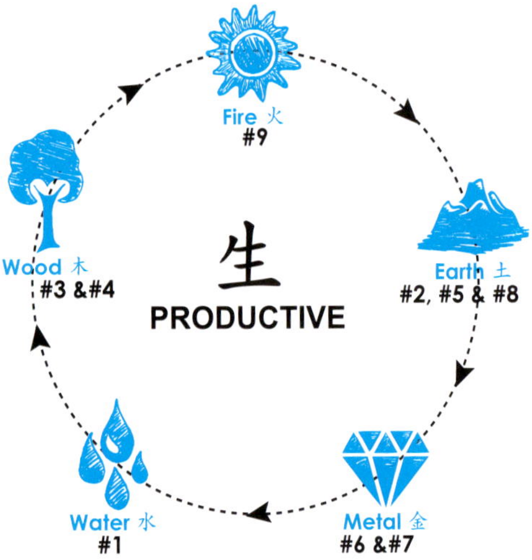

生
PRODUCTIVE

Fire 火
#9

Earth 土
#2, #5 & #8

Metal 金
#6 & #7

Water 水
#1

Wood 木
#3 & #4

In this cycle,

| Water produces Wood |
| Wood produces Fire |
| Fire produces Earth |
| Earth produces Metal |
| Metal produces Water |

This is a cycle where the elements "produce" one another in terms of providing or helping the growth of another. In the case of Water, then, it produces nourishment for trees and plants (i.e. Wood). An element that produces another element means that it strengthens and grows the element that it produces. Here are some simple metaphors might help you visualize this better:

| |
|---|
| Water waters soil, producing Wood |
| Wood makes kindling, producing Fire |
| Fire makes ashes, producing Earth |
| Earth is mined, producing Metal |
| Metal melts, producing Water |

## Controlling Cycle

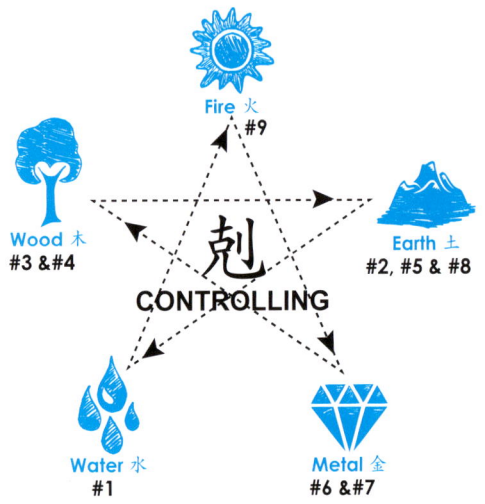

In this cycle,

| Fire controls Metal |
| --- |
| Metal controls Wood |
| Wood controls Earth |
| Earth controls Water |
| Water controls Fire |

This is a cycle where the elements keep each under in "control": an element is countered or subjugated by its controlling element. In this instance, for example, the element of Water controls Fire by putting it out. Here are some simple metaphors to help you visualize it better:

| |
|---|
| Water extinguishes Fire |
| Fire melts Metal |
| Metal cuts Wood |
| Wood roots tightly grip Earth |
| Earth contains Water |

## Weakening Cycle

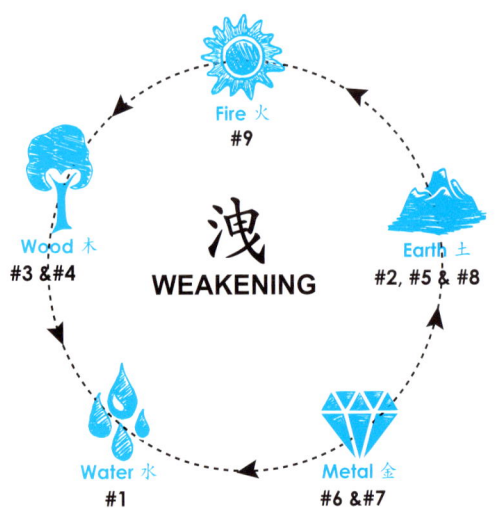

In this cycle,

| Water weakens Metal |
|---|
| Metal weakens Earth |
| Earth weakens Fire |
| Fire weakens Wood |
| Wood weakens Water |

The Weakening Cycle can be best understood as the reverse of the Productive Cycle, in that the strength of the element is weakened by another in order to keep it in check. Remember, the key to Qi in Feng Shui is balance, and different elements keep other elements from becoming too strong. For example, Wood absorbs Water and therefore weakens it. Again, here are some metaphors for easier visualization:

| |
|---|
| Water can be partly absorbed by Wood |
| Wood can be partly burnt by Fire |
| Fire can be diminished with Earth |
| Earth is weakened when mined for Metal |
| Metal is corroded by Water |

The following table shows you the Annual Stars for the year 2000 to 2026.

Examine it and figure out where your room lies; in which sector. Take note of the element of that sector and remember that as a Star 1 person, your element is Water.

### 2002, 2011, 2020

| SE Xun | S Li | SW Kun |
|---|---|---|
| 6 White METAL | 2 Black EARTH | 4 Green WOOD |
| 7 Yellow EARTH | 7 Red METAL | 9 Purple FIRE |
| 1 White WATER | 3 Jade WOOD | 8 White EARTH |
| NE Gen | N Kan | NW Qian |

### 2003, 2012, 2021

| SE Xun | S Li | SW Kun |
|---|---|---|
| 5 Yellow EARTH | 1 White WATER | 3 Jade WOOD |
| 4 Green WOOD | 6 White METAL | 8 White EARTH |
| 9 Purple FIRE | 2 Black EARTH | 7 Red METAL |
| NE Gen | N Kan | NW Qian |

### 2004, 2013, 2022

| SE Xun | S Li | SW Kun |
|---|---|---|
| 4 Green WOOD | 9 Purple FIRE | 2 Black EARTH |
| 3 Jade WOOD | 5 Yellow EARTH | 7 Red METAL |
| 8 White EARTH | 1 White WATER | 6 White METAL |
| NE Gen | N Kan | NW Qian |

### 2005, 2014, 2023

| SE Xun | S Li | SW Kun |
|---|---|---|
| 3 Jade WOOD | 8 White EARTH | 1 White WATER |
| 2 Black EARTH | 4 Green WOOD | 6 White METAL |
| 7 Red METAL | 9 Purple FIRE | 5 Yellow EARTH |
| NE Gen | N Kan | NW Qian |

### 2006, 2015, 2024

| SE Xun | S Li | SW Kun |
|---|---|---|
| 2 Black EARTH | 7 Red METAL | 9 Purple FIRE |
| 1 White WATER | 3 Jade WOOD | 5 Yellow EARTH |
| 6 White EARTH | 8 White EARTH | 4 Green WOOD |
| NE Gen | N Kan | NW Qian |

### 2007, 2016, 2025

| SE Xun | S Li | SW Kun |
|---|---|---|
| 1 White WATER | 6 White METAL | 8 White EARTH |
| 9 Purple FIRE | 2 Black EARTH | 4 Green WOOD |
| 5 Yellow EARTH | 7 Red METAL | 3 Jade WOOD |
| NE Gen | N Kan | NW Qian |

### 2008, 2017, 2026

| SE Xun | S Li | SW Kun |
|---|---|---|
| 9 Purple FIRE | 5 Yellow EARTH | 7 Red METAL |
| 8 White WATER | 1 White WATER | 3 Jade WOOD |
| 4 Green WOOD | 6 White METAL | 2 Black EARTH |
| NE Gen | N Kan | NW Qian |

### 2000, 2009, 2018

| SE Xun | S Li | SW Kun |
|---|---|---|
| 8 White EARTH | 4 Green WOOD | 6 White METAL |
| 7 Red METAL | 9 Purple FIRE | 2 Black EARTH |
| 3 Jade WOOD | 5 Yellow EARTH | 1 White WATER |
| NE Gen | N Kan | NW Qian |

### 2001, 2010, 2019

| SE Xun | S Li | SW Kun |
|---|---|---|
| 7 Red METAL | 3 Jade WOOD | 5 Yellow EARTH |
| 6 White METAL | 8 White EARTH | 1 White WATER |
| 2 Black EARTH | 4 Green WOOD | 9 Purple FIRE |
| NE Gen | N Kan | NW Qian |

These Annual Stars shows you the location of the Stars in a property for the duration of the years specified. Based on the year, the Annual Stars will be located in different sectors of the house. Accordingly, different Annual Stars will affect the Feng Shui of your room in different years.

If the Annual Star of your bedroom is of the same element as your Life Star then the outcome is likely to be prosperous (productive cycle). If the Annual Star is your Life Star's controlling element (controlling cycle), then the result is likely to be stressful – although this combination is still desirable. But if the Annual Star element is the countering element (countering cycle) of your Life Star, then the combination is an unfavorable or inauspicious one for you. (Special note: the #5 yellow Star is generally an undesirable Annual Star for your bedroom regardless of your Life Star.)

Think about the way the element of the Annual Star and your element (Water) interact.

Besides the Annual Stars of the year, there also other factors to be considered. These include the Flying Stars chart of your specific house or property with the Sitting and Facing Stars. Advanced students may want to read *Xuan Kong Flying Stars Feng Shui* for further information. These Stars also affect the evaluation of the impact of the Xuan Kong Flying Stars on your property. There are many other ways of assessing the Feng Shui of a property, and it's important to understand that all these factors play an important and related role.

# Characteristics of Star 1

We all have our "good days" and "bad days". Feng Shui seeks to help isolate why this happens and provide advice that you can use to make every day a "good day" where you are in your element. This section outlines the good and bad characteristics of your Life Star. In a positive sector of your house or work, the positive attributes of your Life Star will be further enhanced, and you will display more of these characteristics. In a negative sector, the positive attributes will be diminished and the negative attributes will begin to show through. Your bad characteristics will take center stage.

# The Good

# Intelligent

As a Star 1 person, one of your key characteristics is intelligence. The Water element is related to wisdom and insight, and thus you are a reflective, deep-thinker. You tend to seek out knowledge and like to surround yourself with people, ideas, books and systems of thought that provide structure to your life and enrich your mind. You are good at observing things and coming up with your own ideas and thoughts.

## Creative

You are incredibly creative, with the unique ability to come up with thoughts and ideas that nobody else can. You discover solutions to problems that aren't always clear-cut or easily visible. This is partly due to your powerful ability to adapt and thinking laterally. You don't allow yourself to be encumbered by norms, rules, and regulations. As such, there is a freedom to your thoughts which enables you to dream big and dream exceptional.

# Intuitive

You're very good at merging with the existing environment. Like water, you adapt to different people and places very well, and you have strong powers of observation and listening skills. As such, you tend to have a large reservoir of "stored" information which you can tap into subconsciously, intuitively making decisions based on a wealth of past experience. You don't simply fumble in the dark, eventually getting things right: instead, you cultivate the necessary talents needed to be able to think fast and make decisions in an innate and perceptive manner.

## Sociable

You can be quite adventurous if the situation suits you, but your sense of sociability is not loud and invasive. Your genuine interest in those around you shines through as you discreetly observe and listen attentively to what others say. Other people respond well to you because of this. You are articulate and sensitive in conversation and cater to the needs of others.

壞

# The Bad

# Vague

Because of your flexibility, you can come off as fairly agreeable in almost all situations, but there are limits to how well this can serve you. Being too flexible can be a sign of weakness and you can become non-committal, indecisive and temperamental with a lack of clear opinions or direction. You may start something with enthusiasm, and then have trouble following up or bringing it to fruition.

## Insecure

You could be thought of as something of a dark horse, playing your cards close to your chest. You keep your thoughts and feelings well-hidden. Sometimes you do this for self preservation but other times you do it to shield yourself from being hurt by others. You often doubt the intentions of others and this tendency to conceal your real feelings in order to avoid getting hurt can damage your personal relationships. Jealousy and suspicion can become issues for you.

# Isolated

Your Lone Ranger tendency can cause you problems if you let it. You can become so wrapped up in keeping others at arms length that they may tire of trying to get close to you, leaving you truly alone when you wish to reach out! Your desire to keep your feelings and thoughts to yourself could become an impediment if you start to lose the ability to share the inner parts of yourself with the people who matter in your life. Confidentiality and privacy can be taken to extremes.

# Scheming

You tend to have a strong sense of pride that it buttressed by the occasional belief that you are superior to everyone else! As such, you can be quite controlling, knowing exactly how you want things to pan out. However, you will be discreet about this, and tend to strategise and scheme in order to get things to work out in your favour. There is a danger that you can become too involved in your own strategising and you may come to care too much about winning and losing instead of the actual experience of something.

# 職業和財富

# CAREER AND WEALTH

# Characteristics at Work

As a Star 1 person, you may display some of these basic characteristics in professional situations at the workplace and in relation to your career. Being aware of your own key characteristics will help you understand why you act and react to situations, people, and tasks in the way you do.

This section outlines the good and bad characteristics of your Life Star. In a positive sector of your house or work, the positive attributes of your Life Star will be further enhanced, and you will display more of these characteristics. In a negative sector, the positive attributes will be diminished and the negative attributes will begin to show through. Your bad characteristics will take center stage.

## • Diplomatic

You have a way with words and a way with people. Your strong listening skills mean that you are excellent at allowing others to share their thoughts and ideas, without cutting in to interrupt with your own comments. This skill means that you can interact well with a wide cross section of people; superiors, colleagues, subordinates, clients, business partners and more all communicate well with you, comfortably.

- ## **Independent**

You are strong and independent. You don't need the affirmation and confirmation of others to make you believe in the merit of your own ideas and put them to good use. As such, others feel comfortable trusting you with big projects and important responsibilities because of your ability to take initiative and act decisively on your own.

- ## **Spontaneous**

You have a good sense of instinct and a strong idea of what feels right. This stems from your natural creativity and fluid intelligence. You don't like to be tied down or hampered by too many limitations, rules, or boundaries but this also means that you lack the ability to properly plan and execute structured plans. You can be disorganized and impatient because you crave spontaneity.

- ## Competitive

You don't like to lose. You feel at your best when you feel that you're ahead of others. On a healthy level, this makes you ambitious and a strong go-getter who won't settle for anything less than success. On the other hand, on an unhealthy level you can be overbearing and aggressive, and may resort to underhand tactics to get ahead. You may sometimes lose sight of the bigger picture in pursuit of a certain goal.

# Suitable Job Roles

- ## Philosopher / professor

You are a deep thinker, and this is where you can put your thinking to good use! You like mental puzzles and don't shy away from challenging thoughts. In fact, you can lose yourself in ideas and knowledge and enjoy reading and expanding your understanding of things around you. Your creativity ensures that you don't accept or tolerate lazy thinking and easy solutions. As such, you can teach philosophy and practice it, or find a way to combine the two in the manner of a public intellectual.

- ## Writer / Communications

You are very verbal and articulate, and this translates into careers that involve lots of writing or speech. You may find that you have a natural talent for creative writing, journalism or copy writing. A job that requires you to communicate with others and that counts on the strength of diplomacy and networking will also work well for you.

- ## Lawyer

This is a career choice combines both mental dexterity and articulation. Your sharp mind likes to probe all corners and explore all perspectives, which is precisely what a lawyer needs to do as they are often required to fight a corner they wouldn't normally stand in. Good lawyers also need to break the bounds of conventional thought in order to make or break a case.

## • Politician

Being both ambitious and adaptive, you are sure to succeed in politics as a politician must be able to come off as likeable and charismatic, while displaying intelligence and gusto in addressing important, contentious issues. You engage well with people, and your drive and keen interest in winning means that you will have the strength and dedication to persevere through the minefield that is politics!

# Career and wealth guide

- ## Keep it interesting

You need to be challenged, and you never back down from an adventure. While you may seem easygoing and affable on the outside, you have a core of strength on the inside that can handle challenges quite well. You will thrive in a job that challenges you. The quickest way to douse your fires is to allow yourself to be stuck in a career that is monotonous, rigid, and predictable.

## • Do not gamble

You have a tendency to want to push things as far as they can go to see how far you can go. This is not always advisable, particularly in matters of wealth. You tend to have indirect wealth luck, which means that you make money from your thoughts and ideas and from side income instead of through full-time salary work. However, while you are good at making money you can also be very extravagant and a spendthrift. You need to work harder to curtail your gambling instincts.

- ## Patience can sometimes be a virtue

Being the type that is unlikely to sit still (or if you do, it's not for long periods of time, or otherwise you become stagnant Water), you need to learn to exercise patience. Certain things simply cannot be rushed or pushed, or they will backfire. This applies to matters of wealth. For example, think long-term investments like property. In business, sometimes you simply have to sit back and wait for the right moment to strike. Patience really is a virtue, one that you would do well to cultivate!

- ## Be proactive

You need to be able to call the shots most of the time, and for that you need some leeway for your creativity and intelligence to flower and bloom. You know how to seek out interesting situations, so appease your sense of independence by going all out to find and explore different things. Do not hold yourself back, boldly grab new opportunities!

- ## Create a structure

While you need to give yourself room to manoeuvre and be free, you also need to reign in your tendency to fly off the handle or chaos could ensue. This applies to your work-related projects and your finances. Some form of discipline goes a long way, whether in terms of a daily schedule or a proper, long-term budget.

**Famous Personalities :**
Sam Walton, Nelson Mandela, James Cameron, Elizabeth Taylor, Martha Stewart

# 人際關係

# RELATIONSHIPS

# Guide for Relationships

As a Star 1 person, you're very tuned in to other people, and as such, others consider you attractive. You're someone worth spending time with because your attentive personality makes other people feel good about themselves. In romance and matters of the heart, you can be quite flirtatious and you are definitely in touch with your sexuality and desires. As such, you tend to enjoy the romance and adventure of multiple love affairs. In the long-term, however, you may have trouble settling down with just one partner. This ties in with your need to be spontaneous and to be continually surprised and challenged all the time.

If a relationship is not going the way you want it to go, you can become insecure and overreact to the smallest thing. Despite your genuine care and concern for the other person, at some level you feel that you must have the upper hand or authority in order to avoid being hurt. Then, you may start to lash out at the other person due to your temper and quickly changing moods. Or, you might hide behind your sense of reserve and become inscrutable to the other person. They will have a hard time knowing what you actually think or feel and this lack of communication and intimacy is poison for many relationships unless you learn to change.

The biggest challenge you face as a Star 1 person is to balance the demands you make of others (such as your partner or spouse) with how much you give of yourself. You are gentle, responsible, and caring, but you may not know when you may be isolating yourself from others by refusing to share your feelings. Furthermore, having high expectations of others and then retreating into suspicion when they don't live up to them will only cause further heartache. You can't retreat and hope to truly become closer to others!

You will have to make an effort to communicate more, but make sure that you communicate the truth of matters with your communication: clarify matters, don't seek to confuse them! Allow yourself to put your heart on the line, show your weakness and have a little faith that you will not get hurt.

You need to strive to be more sincere and honest to your loved ones, and to understand that true intimacy can only come through some measure of consistency in your relations. As a Water element person, there is a tendency for you to flow in and out of trouble and disappear into a cloud when the heat is on, but as long as you make an effort to sit still and be available to the other person in difficult times and arguments, one half of the battle is already won.

**Star 1 in relationships:**
Your easy-going nature make it difficult for you to know where to draw the line, thus may sometimes wind up interesting situations.

# 健康

# HEALTH

# Guide for Health

Body parts and organs that are related to Star 1: Kidneys, bladder, and the reproductive system.

The organs and systems in the body that are likely to cause health problems for you are the kidneys and the urinary system. As a Star 1 person, you are prone to overindulgence (in 'wine, women, and song', as the saying will have it, but this applies to both men and women of this Star!). You tend to enjoy social activities and may indulge in excessive drink which puts a strain on your kidneys and liver. Venereal diseases are also something to guard against.

The weakened immune system you are prone to renders you easily susceptible to colds, flu, and sinus allergies or inflammation of the nose. Your respiratory system is often the victim of attack, and if you are to fall ill you should be aware of these vulnerabilities. Part of your susceptibilities can be explained by the unpredictable nature of your life, and you sometimes neglect to pay attention to your health, diet, and nutrition as your mind is often fixated on other less-mundane things.

You may also frequently get eye infections and so will have to take care of your eyesight. Similarly, blood circulation issues might be a problem for you. constant tingling in your feet and toes after a long period of idleness as well as frequent leg cramping are symptomatic of poor circulation, as are vertigo, dizziness, chilblains, and cold exterminates. If you regularly experience these symptoms, talk to your doctor about what you can do to improve the situation.

**Potential health concerns:**

Depression

Emotional turbulence and mental issues

Injuries arising from falling or slipping

Kidney-related ailments

# COMPATIBILITY WITH OTHER LIFE STARS

This section examines your compatibility as a Star 1 with other people who have the same and different Stars. No person goes through life completely alone. Relationships with others form the bedrock of good career networking. Friendships and relations with loved ones, spouses, partners and family make everything worth while. It is necessary to understand how compatible people with different Stars are to prevent conflict and missed opportunities. Bear in mind that issues of compatibility are not definite or set in stone. There are exceptions to every rule. In addition, **the quality of Feng Shui** in your environment helps dictate whether positive or negative traits in people manifest themselves and thus it weighs in on the quality of your relationships with those people. This section serves as a good guide on your relationships with other people of different Stars.

At a glance, Star 1 people are generally quite incompatible with Star 2, Star 5, and Star 8 people. That is because these stars have a strong Earth element that will counter or control the Water element, and does not bode well for strong, long-term connections. This is especially true in terms of career and profession, particularly if you engage in business partnerships as long-term ventures will prove to be problematic. You can try and improve things, however, by working and interacting in areas that fall within your positive Feng Shui directions.

Your relations with people of Star 3 and 4 are likely to go well, particularly because of your beneficial influence on them. You will be likely to offer guidance, help, and counsel to Star 3 and 4 people and be somewhat of a mentor.

You will enjoy good compatibility with those of Star 6 and 7, while the outcome of your relations with people of Star 9 is not exactly bad or problematic, but somewhat complex.

Star 9 people are likely to be your Noble People, in that they will be your unexpected guardian angels who help you get through a problem or present you with an opportunity to move forward. But because Star 9 is of the Fire element, it is also likely to put out your 'Water', and as such, may diminish your wealth.

Where serious incompatibilities with others arise, you can negate some of the damage by choosing to work and interact in an area of your house that contains a pacifying element, in this case, Earth, because it contains water.

The chart below lists element people or sectors you can utilise to improve your compatibility with other Star people.

|  | Compatibility with others Stars (Individuals) | Seek help from this element people or use this sector |
|---|---|---|
| Star 1 | Star 2, 5 & 8 (Earth Element) | Metal |
| | Star 3 & 4 (wood Element) | Fire |
| | Star 6 & 7 (Metal Element) | Water |
| | Star 9 (Fire Element) | Wood |
| | Star 1 (Water Element) | Earth |

| 巽 SE Xun | 離 S Li | 坤 SW Kun |
|---|---|---|
| **4** Green WOOD | **9** Purple FIRE | **2** Black EARTH |
| **3** Jade WOOD | **5** Yellow EARTH | **7** Red METAL |
| **8** White EARTH | **1** White WATER | **6** White METAL |
| 艮 NE Gen | 坎 N Kan | 乾 NW Qian |

震 E Zhen   兌 W Dui

The following pages will explain in detail the compatibility factor of a Star 1 person with people of all other nine Stars through the Compatibility Meter. The Compatibility Guides give you tips for managing the relationships in question.

| 1 White | compatibility with | 1 White |

## Compatibility Meter

The unfortunate truth is that when you put one Star 1 individual with another Star 1 individual, the two will not be able to truly get along! As deep thinkers and strategists, you will both have very clear – and different – ideas of the way things should be. While you will be civil and take the time to hear the other person out, you both lead life in an almost volatile way; taking risks and making snap decisions in your bid to reach the top. Although you are both socially "fluid", deep down you have a strong ego and even a slight feeling of superiority. This contrasting duality in your natures will create unspoken tension and problems. When you throw in changing temperament then you have a recipe for conflict! You know what you want and so does the other person and this means that you are unlikely to come to any meaningful

compromise or working agreement. You can end up hurting each other because of your thin skins.

## Compatibility Guide

When interacting with another Star 1 person, you will simply need to learn to speak your mind and not lose your temper if you want their to be any chance of progress. If possible, working relationships with another Star 1 person should be avoided because your similarities will make unity nearly impossible. In a romantic context, problems will also arise if left unchecked. While you will be both be in touch with your sexuality, you both have a deep seated fear of getting hurt which can make game playing and power struggles likely. Becoming aware of this reality can help you to overcome it. You must also be aware of both your own or and your partners possible tendency towards over indulgence and possible infidelity if you want a stable relationship. You may have unrealistic expectations of each other so you should be more pragmatic in what you expect from your other half.

| **1** White | compatibility with | **2** Black |

## Compatibility Meter

When you and a Star 2 person get together, you may immediately find that you are incompatible. Although you are both mild mannered, you have some striking differences in your world view and approach to life. You live life at a fast pace, doing things on a whim. You are competitive and driven. Star 2 people are happiest when in their comfort zone: avoiding risks and taking the safe bet to the point of becoming stuck in life. They are patient almost to a fault, occasionally missing out on opportunities which you would have grabbed in a heartbeat. They will see you as rash with an unrealistic world view. It is easy to see how this can cause problems in the workplace; for example, if your boss is a Star 2 person then they may not agree with what they view as

haphazard working methods, even if you get things done. This will frustrate you and can cause you to lose your temper.

## Compatibility Guide

The stagnant and unchanging stance of Star 2 individuals frustrates you. To you, they will seem stubborn and close minded, despite the fact they have a gentle and unassuming nature. Once a Star 2 individual has made up their mind about something it is extremely unlikely that you will be able to change it. This is despite the fact that your diplomatic skills are usually a resounding success. The key to working with such a person is to accept their unchanging nature and not lose your temper when things do not go your way. If a Star 2 person is in charge then you will simply have to adapt to their way of working, despite your hate or rules and regulations. A romantic relationship with a Star 2 individual is likely to be fraught with unhappiness and so it may be a good idea to avoid it.

| **1** White | compatibility with | **3** Jade |

## Compatibility Meter

When you and a Star 3 person get together, the result is likely to be auspicious.

Star 1 and Star 3 individuals will be each other's Noble People, and as such the two of you are likely to help each other out in terms of resolving problems and coming together to find solutions. Your differences complement each other: where you flow freely through situations, a Star 3 individual is rigid and needs a road map. You will, however have a common drive and impatient hunger for success which means that you can make a formidable team, so long as you have the same goal in mind. Your differences will play out in a romantic relationship but they aren't a deal breaker! For example, you can be a positive influence in the life of a Star 3 person because

your spontaneous nature can bring some adventure and excitement into their life that they otherwise would not seek out.

## Compatibility Guide

To make this connection work in the long-term, it will be important for you to give and take and present yourself in a gracious and generous manner to win over the Star 3 person as a strong ally. Star 3 individuals have a strong personality. Unchecked, you tend to go with the flow and agree with others, acting almost like a "yes man". If you do this around a Star 3 person then you will simply find yourself doing their bidding, which is difficult for you as you need to feel in control. Be assertive but don't lose your temper! Having a love for structure, they may also disagree with your working methods in a business situation but you can win them over by showing, as you have shown others, that you can get things done on your own. Whilst they may be aggressive you can use your diplomacy and brilliant mind to help win them over to your methods and way of doing things. In a relationship, compromise is important. They will usually make their desires very clear and you mean have to put your need to be in control to one side and meet them half way in some matters.

| **1** White | compatibility with | **4** White |

## Compatibility Meter

When you and a Star 4 person get together, the outcome will be positive for you. As a Star 1 individual you are likely to meet your new best friend in a Star 4 person. You both share a passion for creative pursuits. A Star 4 person has a strong appreciation of literature and the arts and you may find that this can lead to a productive professional union. Your shared interests lay the groundwork for a strong friendship. When arguments arise, your diplomacy combined with as Star 4 individuals reasonable ability to examine both sides of an argument will mean that conflict is short-lived. Your independence, however, may cause some difficulty in matters of romance as Star 4 individuals can become clingy and dependent in relationships. You like to play your cards close to your chest but Star 4 individuals are the most romantic of all

the Stars and a lack of communication and emotional sharing is not conducive a healthy romantic relationship.

## Compatibility Guide

To make a friendship or relationship with a Star 4 person work, you need to communicate. If in a romantic relationship, be aware that they have a tendency to get "lost" in romance and become too dependant. Your agreeable nature can mean that you can mirror their enthusiasm and find yourself in over your head unless you exercise some caution and composure. You will need to open up to this person in order to get communication flowing because they can be quiet. Things will remain unsaid unless you overcome your tendency to hide your feelings. You also cannot allow yourself to be excessively moody or temperamental when times are tough. Star 4 individuals respond well to reason and temperance and so reason and a level head will win them over. If a Star 4 person senses that you are unreasonable, he or she might start to doubt you and your capabilities which can lead to trouble in the workplace, suffocating any chance of career progression.

| **1** White | compatibility with | **5** Yellow |

## Compatibility Meter

A Star 1 individual and a Star 5 individual are not compatible. The both of you will have very different understanding of the same situation, resulting in constant conflict. Whilst you make the most of random opportunities, living in the moment, Star 5 individuals work to a meticulous plan. They believe there is a time and a place for everything whilst you have an "anything goes" attitude to many things. Star 5 individuals are headstrong, calculative and controlling. None of this is compatible with your sense of independence and indeed, your own ego. In certain negative situations, Star 5 people can be two-faced, and, as you have a sincere interest in others, you will be intolerant of this. This is especially true if this is a business or work-related partnership, as you will find that your trust in the Star 5 person is

easily compromised. You have expectations of others and you will find yourself consistently let down by Star 5 individuals.

## Compatibility Guide

To make your relationship with the Star 5 person work will take quite a lot of work, and whether or not you should try to do so all depends on whether or not you consider the emotional and mental investment a worthwhile one. You will be unable to tolerate the Star 5 person's behaviour if you sense that he or she is occasionally two-faced or prone to changing their tune depending on the situation. It might be better to cut your losses early and move on, if possible. Romantic relationships with a Star 5 person will be strained at best. You value your independence and Star 5 individuals do not need others. Neither of you will encourage growth or happiness in the other. Constant misunderstandings and dissatisfaction will dominate your interactions.

| **1** White | compatibility with | **6** White |

## Compatibility Meter

When Star 1 people get together with Star 6 people, the result is a mutually-beneficial relationship, with great success. Your strengths and weaknesses interact in a harmonious way. Your drive can make up for the tendency that Star 6 individuals have to avoid beginning a project. Their straight talking can mean that problems are always brought out into the open, meaning that resentment or frustration doesn't have the chance to build up when differences exist. Star 6 individuals are perfectionists which means they worry about the small details. You, on the other hand are ideally suited to thinking of the bigger picture. Together you may be able to comprehensively bring grand projects to fruition. Both you and the Star 6 person share a similar sense of confidence and pride, which will work for long-term relationships and partnerships, as one person doesn't always feel overshadowed by another. One problem, however, is that Star 1 and Star 6 people are

equally strong-minded and stubborn, which means that neither will give way when a real argument does arise.

## Compatibility Guide

The two of you are likely to be in a contentious relationship, but this is by no means a bad thing. It only means that you need to learn how to navigate an argument or disagreement so as to not hurt each other or cause lasting damage. During a dispute, it will be necessary for both to take some time apart in order to 'cool down' instead of engaging in a battle of wills. You are both prone to becoming distant, barricading yourselves for fear of getting hurt. Whilst it is good to be aware of this tendency so that you can respect it in one another, it can be taken too far. Learn to communicate your inner feelings more and this will go a long way towards avoiding some conflict in the first place. A Star 6 person is fiercely loyal and they have staying power in business and personal relationships which can help provide you with the patience to stick with things long enough for results to materialize. In a business setting, A Star 6 person may have some difficulty delegating to you as they are used to entrusting work to themselves only, so you must prove to them that you are capable of getting things done.

| **1** White | compatibility with | **7** Red |

## Compatibility Meter

When Star 1 people get together with Star 7 people, the result is a mutually-beneficial if tentative relationship. You both look for a little adventure and you share a taste for the finer side of life. Star 7 individuals may at first seem superficial but underneath, like you, they are observant of others and have a capacity for deep thought. Their bubbly nature means that Star 7 people make interesting friends! Star 7 people will be more than willing to help you out, as they are drawn to your sincerity and honesty in social situations. They can sense that your interest in others is genuine. You may find yourself thinking that they are possibly too smug for their own good and their occasionally aggressive and condescending behaviour is at odds with your quiet, reserved socialising style, but on the

other hand, you should be aware that you yourself are prone to slightly unwarranted pride and self importance.

## Compatibility Guide

There is more to a Star 7 person than meets the eye but their superficial behaviour and vanity can make it initially difficult for you to connect as friends or lovers. In a business environment, however, Star 7 individuals are go getters and so you may be able to forge a productive working relationship with them. You may have to put your own pride to one side and accept that they too have a need to be dominant and the centre of attention. This can be difficult since you also enjoy calling the shots. If this is a romantic relationship, bear in mind that Star 7 people need their sense of space and freedom. Be careful that you do not push them away with too many demands and expectations, borne out of jealousy or paranoia. They are happiest when things are done on their own terms.

| **1** White | compatibility with | **8** White |

## Compatibility Meter

When Star 1 people get together with Star 8 people, the results are damaging. Your similarities mean that conflict slowly brews, in the background. Although both Star 1 and Star 8 people are opinionated and have their own ideas of how things should be, they don't articulate their ideas strongly for fear of conflict. This passive approach to life drives a wedge between Star 1 and Star 8 people and ensures they never directly speak about big issues, instead going over the same problems repeatedly without coming to any kind of conclusions or solutions. You will find yourself unable to change the mind of a Star 8 person once they've made it up, even with your diplomatic skills. You will find yourself striving hard to fulfil the demands of the Star 8 individual, and in a romantic relationship in particular this can build up to long-term resentment and dislike, encouraging

you to recede further into your own company rather than opening up. If this is a work-related connection, then expect to constantly argue with each other over the best way to get something done. In the long run, a falling out may eventually occur.

## Compatibility Guide

Making a connection work with a Star 8 person will take a lot of work. You will have to constantly give in quite a bit to ensure that arguments don't fester and become something worse. This goes against your need to be in control and despite your best efforts, constant, if not abrasive arguments are likely to be a regular turn-of-events for your relationship with a Star 8 person. Such a relationship is likely to cause more problems than happiness. A partnership with Star 8 people is also best avoided as the focus will not be on achieving mutual goals. You will waste valuable energy and time involved in a slow power struggle.

| **1** White | compatibility with | **9** Purple |

## Compatibility Meter

When Star 1 people get together with Star 1 people, the result is tempestuous.

A complex and quite complicated relationship is in store. You may find yourself constantly on your toes: you will never be bored, especially if this is a friendship or a relationship. The unpredictable nature of your interactions sits well with your love of spontaneity! On the other hand, you tend to hold certain expectations of others. It is likely that in a romantic situation you will find yourself expecting certain results which may not come to pass because of the unpredictable nature of your relationship. This can upset you. Keep in mind also that for a partnership or working relationship, the added emotional 'drama' may distract from the work that you have to get done. What makes for an exciting, charged romantic relationship is not ideal for a business one. When all is said and done, the basic attraction between Star 9 and

Star 9 people is strong on many levels so that any conflict between you somehow always ends in reconciliation and forgiveness.

## Compatibility Guide

If a connection between a Star 1 and Star 9 person is to work then it is essential that both parties understand one another, otherwise both of you will be talking past each other instead of at each other. Your diplomatic skill means that you can sometimes avoid saying what you really think simply to avoid conflict and so problems are never brought up, instead growing in the back of your mind. Because your relationship is complex, arguments are at risk of becoming the dominant force in your interactions. Take care to keep your mood swings and argumentative side in check. This is particularly true for a partnership – if you spend too much of time trying to prove the Star 9 person wrong or defending your point of view, you will find that you will be distracted from the more important goals. Pick your fights wisely instead of taking the bait for each and every one and your relationship with a Star 9 person can be healthy, vibrant and even productive, as new ideas will result from your differences.

# About Joey Yap

Joey Yap first began learning about Chinese Metaphysics from masters in the field when he was fifteen.

Despite having graduated with a Commerce degree in Accounting, Joey never became an accountant. Instead, he began to give seminars, talks and professional Chinese Metaphysic consultations in Malaysia, Singapore, India, Australia, Canada, England, Germany and the United States, becoming a household name in the field.

By the age of twenty-six, Joey became a self-made millionaire and in 2008, he was listed in The Malaysian Tatler as the Top 300 Most Influential People in Malaysia and Prestige's Top 40 Under 40.

His practical and result-driven take on Feng Shui and BaZi sets him apart from other older, traditional masters and practitioners in the field. He shows people how the ancient teachings can be utilized for tangible REAL world benefits. The success he and his clients enjoy, thanks to his advice, is positive proof that Feng Shui and BaZi Astrology works, whether everyone believes in it or not!

Today, Joey has helped and worked with governments and the wealthiest people in Singapore, Hong Kong, China, Malaysia and Japan. His clients include multinationals, developers, tycoons and royalties. On Bloomberg, he is featured on-air as a regular guest on the subject of Feng Shui annual forecasts. He is retained by twenty-five top Malaysian property developers to help determine suitable candidates to take top management, change their space and Feng Shui mechanism, the way they make decisions, and understand the natural cosmic energies that can influence their decision-making.

Every year he conducts his 'Feng Shui and Astrology' seminar to a crowd of more than 3500 people at the Kuala Lumpur Convention Center. He also takes this annual seminar on a world tour to Frankfurt, San Francisco, New York, Las Vegas, Toronto, Sydney and Singapore.

The Joey Yap Consulting Group is the world's largest and first specialized metaphysics consultation firm. His consultancy, and professional speaking and training engagements with Microsoft, HP, Bloomberg, Citibank, HSBC and many more have seen the benefits of Classical Feng Shui and BaZi find their way into corporate environment and culture. Celebrities, property developers and other large organizations turn to Joey when they need the best.

After years of field-testing and fine-tuning his teachings, he has put together a team in the form of Joey Yap Research International. The objective of this Research Team is to scientifically track and verify the positive impact of Feng Shui and BaZi on subjects and ultimately to assist more people in achieving their life goals.

The Mastery Academy of Chinese Metaphysics which Joey founded teaches thousands of students from all around the world about Classical Feng Shui, Chinese Astrology and Face Reading. Many graduates have gone on to become successful in their own right, becoming sought after consultants, setting up their own consultancy businesses or even becoming educators, passing on Chinese Metaphysics knowledge to others.

Joey has also created the Decision Referential Technology™, offering decision reformation training on how to make better decisions in business and in personal life. He has led his team of highly trained consultants to help clients create more positive change in corporate boardrooms and increase production in their companies, helping people see their business outlook for each year so they may anticipate, plan and execute their strategies successfully.

Joey's work has been featured regularly in various popular global publications and networks like Time, Forbes, the International Herald Tribune and Bloomberg. He has also written columns for The New Straits Times, The Star and The Edge – Malaysia's leading newspapers. He has achieved bestselling author status with over sixty-five books, which have sold more than three million copies to-date.

His success is not limited to matters of Feng Shui and BaZi. Although his success is a product of them, he is also a successful entrepreneur, leading his own companies and property investment portfolio. When not teaching metaphysics or consulting around the world, Joey is a Naruto-fan, avid snowboarder and is crazy for fruits de mer.

Author's personal website :

 **www.joeyyap.com**

Joey Yap on Facebook:

 **www.facebook.com/JoeyYapFB**

# MASTERY ACADEMY
## OF CHINESE METAPHYSICS
### Your **Preferred** Choice to the Art & Science of Classical Chinese Metaphysics Studies

Bringing **innovative** techniques
and **creative** teaching methods
to an ancient study.

**Mastery Academy of Chinese Metaphysics** was established by Joey Yap to play the role of disseminating this Eastern knowledge to the modern world with the belief that this valuable knowledge should be accessible to anyone, anywhere.

Its goal is to enrich people's lives through accurate, professional teaching and practice of Chinese Metaphysics knowledge globally. It is the first academic institution of its kind in the world to adopt the tradition of Western institutions of higher learning - where students are encourage to explore, question and challenge themselves and to respect different fields and branches of study - with the appreciation and respect of classical ideas and applications that have stood the test of time.

The art and science of Chinese Metaphysics studies – be it Feng Shui, BaZi (Astrology), Mian Xiang (Face Reading), ZeRi (Date Selection) or Yi Jing – is no longer a field shrouded with mystery and superstition. In light of new technology, fresher interpretations and innovative methods as well as modern teaching tools like the Internet, interactive learning, e-learning and distance learning, anyone from virtually any corner of the globe, who is keen to master these disciplines can do so with ease and confidence under the guidance and support of the Academy.

It has indeed proven to be a center of educational excellence for thousands of students from over thirty countries across the world; many of whom have moved on to practice classical Chinese Metaphysics professionally in their home countries.

At the Academy, we believe in enriching people's lives by empowering their destinies through the disciplines of Chinese Metaphysics. Learning is not an option - it's a way of life!

MASTERY ACADEMY
OF CHINESE METAPHYSICS™

**MALAYSIA**
19-3, The Boulevard, Mid Valley City, 59200 Kuala Lumpur, Malaysia
Tel : +603-2284 8080   |   Fax : +603-2284 1218
Email     : info@masteryacademy.com
Website  : www.masteryacademy.com

Australia, Austria, Canada, China, Croatia, Cyprus, Czech Republic, Denmark, France, Germany, Greece, Hungary, India, Italy, Kazakhstan, Malaysia, Netherlands (Holland), New Zealand, Philippines, Poland, Russian Federation, Singapore, Slovenia, South Africa, Switzerland, Turkey, U.S.A., Ukraine, United Kingdom

www.masteryacademy.com   |   +603 - 2284 8080

# Mastery Academy around the world

# JOEY YAP CONSULTING GROUP

## Pioneering Metaphysics - Centric Personal Coaching and Corporate Consulting

The Joey Yap Consulting Group is the world's first specialised metaphysics consultation firm. Founded in 2002 by renown international Feng Shui and BaZi consultant, author and trainer Joey Yap, the Joey Yap Consulting Group is a pioneer in the provision of metaphysics-driven coaching and consultation services for individuals and corporations.

The Group's core consultation practice areas are Feng Shui and BaZi, which are complimented by ancillary services like Date Selection, Face Reading and Yi Jing Divination. The Group's team of highly-trained professional consultants are led by Principal Consultant Joey Yap. The Joey Yap Consulting Group is the firm of choice for corporate captains, entrepreneurs, celebrities and property developers when it comes to Feng Shui and BaZi-related advisory and knowledge.

## Across Industries: Our Portfolio of Clients

Our diverse portfolio of both corporate and individual clients from all around the world bears testimony to our experience and capabilities.

Joey Yap Consulting Group is the firm of choice for many of Asia's leading multi-national corporations, listed entities, conglomerates and top-tier property developers when it comes to Feng Shui and corporate BaZi.

Our services also engaged by professionals, prominent business personalities, celebrities, high-profile politicians and people from all walks of life.

---

## JOEY YAP CONSULTING GROUP

Name (Mr./Mrs./Ms.): _____

Contact Details

Tel: _____ Fax: _____

Mobile : _____

E-mail: _____

What Type of Consultation Are You Interested In?
☐ Feng Shui  ☐ BaZi  ☐ Date Selection  ☐ Corporate Events

Please tick if applicable:
☐ Are you a Property Developer looking to engage Joey Yap Consulting Group?

☐ Are you a Property Investor looking for tailor-made packages to suit your investment requirements?

Please attach your name card here.

Thank you for completing this form. Please fax it back to us at:

Malaysia & the rest of the world
Fax : +603-2284 2213   Tel : +603-2284 1213

www.joeyyap.com

## Feng Shui Consultations

### For Residential Properties
- Initial Land/Property Assessment
- Residential Feng Shui Consultations
- Residential Land Selection
- End-to-End Residential Consultation

### For Commercial Properties
- Initial Land/Property Assessment
- Commercial Feng Shui Consultations
- Commercial Land Selection
- End-to-End Commercial Consultation

### For Property Developers
- End-to-End Consultation
- Post-Consultation Advisory Services
- Panel Feng Shui Consultant

### For Property Investors
- Your Personal Feng Shui Consultant
- Tailor-Made Packages

### For Memorial Parks & Burial Sites
- Yin House Feng Shui

## BaZi Consultations

### Personal Destiny Analysis
- Personal Destiny Analysis for Individuals
- Children's BaZi Analysis
- Family BaZi Analysis

### Strategic Analysis for Corporate Organizations
- Corporate BaZi Consultations
- BaZi Analysis for Human Resource Management

### Entrepreneurs & Business Owners
- BaZi Analysis for Entrepreneurs

### Career Pursuits
- BaZi Career Analysis

### Relationships
- Marriage and Compatibility Analysis
- Partnership Analysis

### For Everyone
- Annual BaZi Forecast
- Your Personal BaZi Coach

## Date Selection Consultations

- **Marriage Date Selection**
- **Caesarean Birth Date Selection**
- **House-Moving Date Selection**
- **Renovation & Groundbreaking Dates**
- **Signing of Contracts**
- **Official Openings**
- **Product Launches**

## Corporate Events

Many reputable organizations and institutions have worked closely with Joey Yap Consulting Group to build a synergistic business relationship by engaging our team of consultants, led by Joey Yap, as speakers at their corporate events.

We tailor our seminars and talks to suit the anticipated or pertinent group of audience. Be it department, subsidiary, your clients or even the entire corporation, we aim to fit your requirements in delivering the intended message(s).

Tel: +603-2284 1213   Email: consultation@joeyyap.com

# Chinese Metaphysics Reference Series

**The Chinese Metaphysics Reference Series** is a collection of reference texts, source material, and educational textbooks to be used as supplementary guides by scholars, students, researchers, teachers and practitioners of Chinese Metaphysics.

These comprehensive and structured books provide fast, easy reference to aid in the study and practice of various Chinese Metaphysics subjects including Feng Shui, BaZi, Yi Jing, Zi Wei, Liu Ren, Ze Ri, Ta Yi, Qi Men and Mian Xiang.

## The Chinese Metaphysics Compendium

At over 1,000 pages, the *Chinese Metaphysics Compendium* is a unique one-volume reference book that compiles all the formulas relating to Feng Shui, BaZi (Four Pillars of Destiny), Zi Wei (Purple Star Astrology), Yi Jing (I-Ching), Qi Men (Mystical Doorways), Ze Ri (Date Selection), Mian Xiang (Face Reading) and other sources of Chinese Metaphysics.

It is presented in the form of easy-to-read tables, diagrams and reference charts, all of which are compiled into one handy book. This first-of-its-kind compendium is presented in both English and the original Chinese, so that none of the meanings and contexts of the technical terminologies are lost.

The only essential and comprehensive reference on Chinese Metaphysics, and an absolute must-have for all students, scholars, and practitioners of Chinese Metaphysics.

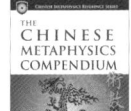

The Ten Thousand Year Calendar (Pocket Edition)

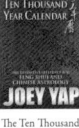
The Ten Thousand Year Calendar

Dong Gong Date Selection

The Date Selection Compendium

Plum Blossoms Divination Reference Book

San Yuan Dragon Gate Eight Formations Water Method

Xuan Kong Da Gua Ten Thousand Year Calendar

Bazi Hour Pillar Useful Gods - Wood

Bazi Hour Pillar Useful Gods - Fire

Bazi Hour Pillar Useful Gods - Earth

Bazi Hour Pillar Useful Gods - Metal

Bazi Hour Pillar Useful Gods - Water

Xuan Kong Da Gua Structures Reference Book

Xuan Kong Da Gua 64 Gua Transformation Analysis

Bazi Structures and Structural Useful Gods - Wood

Bazi Structures and Structural Useful Gods - Fire

Bazi Structures and Structural Useful Gods - Earth

Bazi Structures and Structural Useful Gods - Metal

Bazi Structures and Structural Useful Gods - Water

Xuan Kong Purple White Script

Earth Study Discern Truth Second Edition

www.masteryacademy.com | +603 - 2284 8080

# Joey Yap's BaZi Profiling System

## Three Levels of BaZi Profiling (English & Chinese versions)

In BaZi Profiling, there are three levels that reflect three different stages of a person's personal nature and character structure.

### Level 1 – The Day Master

The Day Master in a nutshell is the BASIC YOU. The inborn personality. It is your essential character. It answers the basic question "WHO AM I". There are ten basic personality profiles – the TEN Day Masters – each with its unique set of personality traits, likes and dislikes.

### Level 2 – The Structure

The Structure is your behavior and attitude – in other words, how you use your personality. It expands on the Day Master (Level 1). The structure reveals your natural tendencies in life – are you more controlling, more of a creator, supporter, thinker or connector? Each of the Ten Day Masters express themselves differently through the FIVE Structures. Why do we do the things we do? Why do we like the things we like? – The answers are in our BaZi STRUCTURE.

### Level 3 – The Profile

The Profile reveals your unique abilities and skills, the masks that you consciously and unconsciously "put on" as you approach and navigate the world. Your Profile speaks of your ROLES in life. There are TEN roles – or Ten BaZi Profiles. Everyone plays a different role.

What makes you happy and what does success mean to you is different to somebody else. Your sense of achievement and sense of purpose in life is unique to your Profile. Your Profile will reveal your unique style.

The path of least resistance to your success and wealth can only be accessed once you get into your "flow." Your BaZi Profile reveals how you can get FLOW. It will show you your patterns in work, relationship and social settings. Being AWARE of these patterns is your first step to positive Life Transformation.

**www.baziprofiling.com**

# BaZi Collections

Leading Chinese Astrology Master Trainer Joey Yap makes it easy to learn how to unlock your Destiny through your BaZi with these books. BaZi or Four Pillars of Destiny is an ancient Chinese science which enables individuals to understand their personality, hidden talents and abilities as well as their luck cycle, simply by examining the information contained within their birth data.

Understand and appreciate more about this astoundingly accurate ancient Chinese Metaphysical science with this BaZi Collection.

## Feng Shui Collection

### Must-Haves for Property Analysis!

For homeowners, those looking to build their own home or even investors who are looking to apply Feng Shui to their homes, these series of books provides valuable information from the classical Feng Shui therioes and applications.

In his trademark straight-to-the-point manner, Joey shares with you the Feng Shui do's and dont's when it comes to finding a property with favorable Feng Shui, which is condusive for home living.

### Stories & Lessons on Feng Shui Series

All in all, this series is a delightful chronicle of Joey's articles, thoughts and vast experience - as a professional Feng Shui consultant and instructor - that have been purposely refined, edited and expanded upon to make for a light-hearted, interesting yet educational read. And with Feng Shui, BaZi, Mian Xiang and Yi Jing all thrown into this one dish, there's something for everyone.

www.masteryacademy.com | +603 - 2284 8080

# Continue Your Journey with Joey Yap Books in Feng Shui

### Pure Feng Shui
Pure Feng Shui is Joey Yap's debut with an international publisher, CICO Books, and is a refreshing and elegant look at the intricacies of Classical Feng Shui – now compiled in a useful manner for modern-day readers. This book is a comprehensive introduction to all the important precepts and techniques of Feng Shui practice.

---

### Your Aquarium Here
This book is the first in Fengshuilogy Series, a series of matter-in-fact and useful Feng Shui books designed for the person who wants to do a fuss-free Feng Shui.

---

### Xuan Kong Flying Stars
This book is an essential introductory book to the subject of Xuan Kong Fei Xing, a well-known and popular system of Feng Shui. Learn 'tricks of the trade' and 'trade secrets' to enhance and maximize Qi in your home or office.

---

### Walking the Dragons
Compiled in one book for the first time from Joey Yap's Feng Shui Mastery Excursion Series, the book highlights China's extensive, vibrant history with astute observations on the Feng Shui of important sites and places. Learn the landform formations of Yin Houses (tombs and burial places), as well as mountains, temples, castles, and villages.

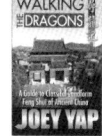

---

### The Art of Date Selection: Personal Date Selection
With the *Art of Date Selection: Personal Date Selection*, learn simple, practical methods you can employ to select not just good dates, but personalized good dates. Whether it's a personal activity such as a marriage or professional endeavor such as launching a business, signing a contract or even acquiring assets, this book will show you how to pick the good dates and tailor them to suit the activity in question, as well as avoid the negative ones too!

---

www.masteryacademy.com  |  +603 - 2284 8080

# Face Reading Collection

## Discover Face Reding (English & Chinese versions)

This is a comprehensive book on all areas of Face Reading, covering some of the most important facial features, including the forehead, mouth, ears and even philtrum above your lips. This book eill help you analyse not just your Destiny but help you achieve your full potential and achieve life fulfillment.

## Joey Yap's Art of Face Reading

The Art of Face Reading is Joey Yap's second effort with CICO Books, and takes a lighter, more practical approach to Face Reading. This book does not so much focus on the individual features as it does on reading the entire face. It is about identifying common personality types and characters.

## Easy Guide on Face Reading (English & Chinese versions)

The Face Reading Essentials series of books comprises 5 individual books on the key features of the face – Eyes, Eyebrows, Ears, Nose, and Mouth. Each book provides a detailed illustration and a simple yet descriptive explanation on the individual types of the features.

The books are equally useful and effective for beginners, enthusiasts, and the curious. The series is designed to enable people who are new to Face Reading to make the most of first impressions and learn to apply Face Reading skills to understand the personality and character of friends, family, co-workers, and even business associates.

## Annual Releases
2011 Annual Outlook & Tong Shu

| Chinese Astrology for 2011 | Feng Shui for 2011 | Tong Shu Desktop Calendar 2011 | Professional Tong Shu Diary 2011 | Tong Shu Monthly Planner 2011 | Weekly Tong Shu Diary 2011 |

www.masteryacademy.com | +603 - 2284 8080

# Educational Tools and Software

## Xuan Kong Flying Stars Feng Shui Software
**The Essential Application for Enthusiasts and Professionals**

The Xuan Kong Flying Stars Feng Shui Software will assist you in the practice of Xuan Kong Feng Shui with minimum fuss and maximum effectiveness. Superimpose the Flying Stars charts over your house plans (or those of your clients) to clearly demarcate the 9 Palaces. Use it to help you create fast and sophisticated chart drawings and presentations, as well as to assist professional practitioners in the report-writing process before presenting the final reports for your clients. Students can use it to practice their Xuan Kong Feng Shui skills and knowledge, and it can even be used by designers and architects!

---

## BaZi Ming Pan Software Version 2.0
**Professional Four Pillars Calculator for Destiny Analysis**

The BaZi Ming Pan Version 2.0 Professional Four Pillars Calculator for Destiny Analysis is the most technically advanced software of its kind in the world today. It allows even those without any knowledge of BaZi to generate their own BaZi Charts, and provides virtually every detail required to undertake a comprehensive Destiny Analysis.

This Professional Four Pillars Calculator allows you to even undertake a day-to-day analysis of your Destiny. What's more, all BaZi Charts generated by this software are fully printable and configurable! Designed for both enthusiasts and professional practitioners, this state-of-the-art software blends details with simplicity, and is capable of generating 4 different types of BaZi charts: **BaZi Professional Charts, BaZi Annual Analysis Charts, BaZi Pillar Analysis Charts and BaZi Family Relationship Charts.**

---

## Joey Yap Feng Shui Template Set

Directions are the cornerstone of any successful Feng Shui audit or application. The **Joey Yap Feng Shui Template Set** is a set of three templates to simplify the process of taking directions and determining locations and positions, whether it's for a building, a house, or an open area such as a plot of land, all with just a floor plan or area map.

The Set comprises 3 basic templates: The Basic Feng Shui Template, 8 Mansions Feng Shui Template, and the Flying Stars Feng Shui Template.

## Mini Feng Shui Compass

The Mini Feng Shui Compass is a self-aligning compass that is not only light at 100gms but also built sturdily to ensure it will be convenient to use anywhere. The rings on the Mini Feng Shui Compass are bi-lingual and incorporate the 24 Mountain Rings that is used in your traditional Luo Pan.

The comprehensive booklet included will guide you in applying the 24 Mountain Directions on your Mini Feng Shui Compass effectively and the 8 Mansions Feng Shui to locate the most auspicious locations within your home, office and surroundings. You can also use the Mini Feng Shui Compass when measuring the direction of your property for the purpose of applying Flying Stars Feng Shui.

www.masteryacademy.com | +603 - 2284 8080

# Educational Tools and Software

## Xuan Kong Vol.1
### An Advanced Feng Shui Home Study Course

Learn the Xuan Kong Flying Star Feng Shui system in just 20 lessons! Joey Yap's specialised notes and course work have been written to enable distance learning without compromising on the breadth or quality of the syllabus. Learn at your own pace with the same material students in a live class would use. The most comprehensive distance learning course on Xuan Kong Flying Star Feng Shui in the market. Xuan Kong Flying Star Vol.1 comes complete with a special binder for all your course notes.

## Feng Shui for Period 8 - (DVD)

Don't miss the Feng Shui Event of the next 20 years! Catch Joey Yap LIVE and find out just what Period 8 is all about. This DVD boxed set zips you through the fundamentals of Feng Shui and the impact of this important change in the Feng Shui calendar. Joey's entertaining, conversational style walks you through the key changes that Period 8 will bring and how to tap into Wealth Qi and Good Feng Shui for the next 20 years.

## Xuan Kong Flying Stars Beginners Workshop - (DVD)

Take a front row seat in Joey Yap's Xuan Kong Flying Stars workshop with this unique LIVE RECORDING of Joey Yap's Xuan Kong Flying Stars Feng Shui workshop, attended by over 500 people. This DVD program provides an effective and quick introduction of Xuan Kong Feng Shui essentials for those who are just starting out in their study of classical Feng Shui. Learn to plot your own Flying Star chart in just 3 hours. Learn 'trade secret' methods, remedies and cures for Flying Stars Feng Shui. This boxed set contains 3 DVDs and 1 workbook with notes and charts for reference.

## BaZi Four Pillars of Destiny Beginners Workshop - (DVD)

Ever wondered what Destiny has in store for you? Or curious to know how you can learn more about your personality and inner talents? BaZi or Four Pillars of Destiny is an ancient Chinese science that enables us to understand a person's hidden talent, inner potential, personality, health and wealth luck from just their birth data. This specially compiled DVD set of Joey Yap's BaZi Beginners Workshop provides a thorough and comprehensive introduction to BaZi. Learn how to read your own chart and understand your own luck cycle. This boxed set contains 3 DVDs and 1 workbook with notes and reference charts.

www.masteryacademy.com | +603 - 2284 8080

# DVD Series

## Joey Yap's Face Reading Revealed DVD Series

Mian Xiang, the Chinese art of Face Reading, is an ancient form of physiognomy and entails the use of the face and facial characteristics to evaluate key aspects of a person's life, luck and destiny. In his Face Reading DVDs series, Joey Yap shows you how the facial features reveal a wealth of information about a person's luck, destiny and personality.

Mian Xiang also tell us the talents, quirks and personality of an individual. Do you know that just by looking at a person's face, you can ascertain his or her health, wealth, relationships and career? Let Joey Yap show you how the 12 Palaces can be utilised to reveal a person's inner talents, characteristics and much more.

## Feng Shui for Homebuyers DVD Series

In these DVDs, you will also learn how to identify properties with good Feng Shui features that will help you promote a fulfilling life and achieve your full potential. Discover how to avoid properties with negative Feng Shui that can bring about detrimental effects to your health, wealth and relationships.

Joey will also elaborate on how to fix the various aspects of your home that may have an impact on the Feng Shui of your property and give pointers on how to tap into the positive energies to support your goals.

## Discover Feng Shui with Joey Yap: Set of 4 DVDs
## Informative and entertaining, classical Feng Shui comes alive in *Discover Feng Shui with Joey Yap!*

You have the questions. Now let Joey personally answer them in this 4-set DVD compilation! Learn how to ensure the viability of your residence or workplace, Feng Shui-wise, without having to convert it into a Chinese antiques' shop. Classical Feng Shui is about harnessing the natural power of your environment to improve quality of life. It's a systematic and subtle metaphysical science.

## Walking the Dragons with Joey Yap (The TV Series)

This DVD set features eight episodes, covering various landform Feng Shui analyses and applications from Joey Yap as he and his co-hosts travel through China. It includes case studies of both modern and historical sites with a focus on Yin House (burial places) Feng Shui and the tombs of the Qing Dynasty emperors.

The series was partly filmed on-location in mainland China, and the state of Selangor, Malaysia.

# Home Study Courses

Gain Valuable Knowledge from the Comfort of Your Home

Now, armed with your trusty computer or laptop and Internet access, knowledge of Chinese Metaphysics is just a click away!

## 3 easy steps to activate your Home Study Course:

**Step 1:**
Go to the URL as indicated on the Activation Card, and key in your Activation Code

**Step 2:**
At the Registration page, fill in the details accordingly to enable us to generate your Student Identification (Student ID).

**Step 3:**
Upon successful registration, you may begin your lessons immediately.

### Joey Yap's Feng Shui Mastery HomeStudy Course

Module 1: **Empowering Your Home**
Module 2: **Master Practitioner Program**

Learn how easy it is to harness the power of the environment to promote health, wealth and prosperity in your life. The knowledge and applications of Feng Shui will no more be a mystery but a valuable tool you can master on your own.

### Joey Yap's BaZi Mastery HomeStudy Course

Module 1: **Mapping Your Life**
Module 2: **Mastering Your Future**

Discover your path of least resistance to success with insights about your personality and capabilities, and what strengths you can tap on to maximize your potential for success and happiness by mastering BaZi (Chinese Astrology). This course will teach you all the essentials you need to interpret a BaZi chart and more.

### Joey Yap's Mian Xiang Mastery HomeStudy Course

Module 1: **Face Reading**
Module 2: **Advanced Face Reading**

A face can reveal so much about a person. Now, you can learn the art and science of Mian Xiang (Chinese Face Reading) to understand a person's character based on his or her facial features with ease and confidence.

www.masteryacademy.com | +603 - 2284 8080

# Feng Shui Mastery™
## LIVE COURSES (MODULES ONE TO FOUR)

The Feng Shui Mastery™ comprises Feng Shui Mastery Modules 1, 2, 3 and 4. It starts off with a foundation program up to the advanced practitioner level. It is a thorough, comprehensive program that covers important theories from various classical Feng Shui systems including Ba Zhai, San Yuan, San He, and Xuan Kong.

**Module One:** Beginners Course  **Module Two:** Practitioners Course  **Module Three:** Advanced Practitioners Course  **Module Four:** Master Course

# BaZi Mastery™
## LIVE COURSES (MODULES ONE TO FOUR)

The BaZi Mastery™ consists of BaZi Mastery Modules 1, 2, 3 and 4. In Modules 1 and 2, students will receive a thorough introduction to BaZi, along with an intensive understanding of BaZi principles and the requisite skills to practice it with accuracy and precision. This will prepare them, and serious Feng Shui practitioners, for a more advanced levels and fine-tune their application skills in Modules 3 and 4.

**Module One:** Intensive Foundation Course  **Module Two:** Practitioners Course  **Module Three:** Advanced Practitioners Course  **Module Four:** Master Course in BaZi

# Xuan Kong Mastery™
## LIVE COURSES (MODULES ONE TO THREE)
\* Advanced Courses For Master Practitioners

The Xuan Kong Mastery™ comprises Xuan Kong Mastery Modules 1, 2A, 2B and 3. It is a sophisticated branch of Feng Shui replete with many techniques and formulae, enabling practitioners to evaluate Feng Shui on a more thorough and in-depth basis. The study of Xuan Kong encompasses numerology, symbology and science of the Ba Gua along with the mathematics of time.

**Module One:** Advanced Foundation Course  **Module Two A:** Advanced Xuan Kong Methodologies  **Module Two B:** Purple White  **Module Three:** Advanced Xuan Kong Da Gua

www.masteryacademy.com  |  +603 - 2284 8080

# Mian Xiang Mastery™
## LIVE COURSES (MODULES ONE AND TWO)

The Mian Xiang Mastery™ comprises of Mian Xiang Mastery Modules 1 and 2 to allow students to learn this ancient art in a thorough, detailed manner. Each module has a carefully-developed syllabus that allows students to get acquainted with the fundamentals of Mian Xiang before moving on to the more intricate theories and principles that will enable them to practice Mian Xiang with greater depth and complexity.

**Module One:**
Basic Face Reading

**Module Two:**
Practical Face Reading

# Yi Jing Mastery™
## LIVE COURSES (MODULES ONE AND TWO)

The Yi Jing Mastery™ comprises Modules 1 and 2. Both Modules aim to give casual and serious Yi Jing enthusiasts a serious insight into one of the most important philosophical treatises in ancient Chinese thought. Yi Jing uses sophisticated formulas and calculations to derive the answers to questions we pose. It is a science of divination, and in our classes there is a heavy emphasis on the scientific aspect of it. It bears no religious or superstitious affiliation.

**Module One:**
Traditional Yi Jing

**Module Two:**
Plum Blossom Numerology

# Ze Ri Mastery™
## LIVE COURSES (MODULES ONE AND TWO)

The ZeRi Mastery™ consists of ZeRi Mastery Modules 1 and 2. This program provides students with a thorough introduction to the art of Date Selection both for Personal and Feng Shui purposes. Our ZeRi Mastery™ aims to provide a thorough and comprehensive program on the art of Date Selection, covering everything from Personal and Feng Shui Date Selection to Xuan Kong Da Gua Date Selection.

**Module One:**
Personal and Feng Shui Date Selection

**Module Two:**
Xuan Kong Da Gua Date Selection

www.masteryacademy.com | +603 - 2284 8080

### Feng Shui for Life

This is an entry-level five-day course designed for the Feng Shui beginner to learn the application of practical Feng Shui in day-to-day living. Lessons include quick tips on analyzing the BaZi chart, simple Feng Shui solutions for the home, basic Date Selection, useful Face Reading techniques and practical Water formulas. A great introduction course on Chinese Metaphysics studies for beginners.

### Joey Yap's
### Design Your Destiny

This is a three-day life transformation program designed to inspire awareness and action for you to create a better quality of life. It introduces the DRT™ (Decision Referential Technology) method, which utilizes the BaZi Personality Profiling system to determine the right version of you, and serves as a tool to help you make better decisions and achieve a better life in the least resistant way possible based on your Personality Profile Type.

## Walk the Mountains! Learn Feng Shui in a Practical and Hands-on Program

###  Feng Shui Mastery Excursion™

Learn landform (Luan Tou) Feng Shui by walking the mountains and chasing the Dragon's vein in China. This Program takes the students in a study tour to examine notable Feng Shui landmarks, mountains, hills, valleys, ancient palaces, famous mansions, houses and tombs in China. The Excursion is a 'practical' hands-on course where students are shown to perform readings using the formulas they've learnt and to recognize and read Feng Shui Landform (Luan Tou) formations.

Read about China Excursion here:
**http://www.fengshuiexcursion.com**

Mastery Academy courses are conducted around the world. Find out when will Joey Yap be in your area by visiting **www.masteryacademy.com** or call our office at **+603-2284 8080**.

www.masteryacademy.com | +603 - 2284 8080